THE JOY of reading
is a blessing forever.
For through good books,
the imagination is enlivened,
wisdom is gained,
and wondrous experiences
bring new fascination to life.

FROM THE LIBRARY OF

SunFlower

CAUGHT IN A HIGHER *Love*

CAUGHT IN A HIGHER

Inspiring Stories
of Women
in the Bible

CAROLYN NABORS BAKER

BROADMAN
& HOLMAN
PUBLISHERS
Nashville, Tennessee

0-8054-1198-4

Published by Broadman & Holman Publishers, Nashville, Tennessee
Acquisitions & Development Editor: William D. Watkins
Cover & inside page design: Anderson Thomas Design
Typesetting: SL Editorial Services, Brentwood, Tennessee

Dewey Decimal Classification: 220.9
Subject Heading: WOMEN IN THE BIBLE
Library of Congress Card Catalog Number: 98-18641

Unless otherwise noted, Scripture quotations are from the Holy Bible,
New International Version, copyright © 1973, 1978, 1984 by
International Bible Society.

Library of Congress Cataloging-in-Publication Data
Baker, Carolyn Nabors.
    Caught in a higher love : inspiring stories of women in the
Bible / by Carolyn Nabors Baker.
        p. cm.
    ISBN 0-8054-1198-4
    1. Women in the Bible—Biography. 2. Women in the Bible—
Meditations. I. Title.
BS575.B27   1998
220.9'2'082—dc21

                                     98-18641
                                         CIP

1 2 3 4 5 02 01 00 99 98

To Lyn, Laura, Rob, and Christian
for your love, encouragement, and
inspiration.

Contents

Acknowledgments

I am deeply grateful for those of you who gave so generously of your time in helping me finalize the writing of this book.

I want to thank the dear friends who were willing to read and offer helpful comments on early drafts: Emily Freeman, Barbara Enkema, Diane Moore, and Landon Saunders.

I also want to thank Linda Qualls for her preparation of the manuscript, and Chaz Corzine of Blanton Harrell Entertainment and Sara Fortenberry, my literary agent, for helping to make this book possible.

I especially want to thank Bill Watkins and the entire editorial team at Broadman & Holman Publishers for their enthusiasm for this book and their careful attention to the entire editorial process.

I'm grateful to my family—Lyn, Laura, Rob, Christian, and Don—for believing in me and for their constant encouragement.

I'm grateful for those of you who have chosen to spend time reading these pages. My prayer is that you will find them helpful in your own journey of faith.

Most of all, I am grateful to the one who has caught me in his love and brought these pages to life.

Introduction

While I have written this book to honor and encourage young women everywhere, especially those in my family and my college classes over the years, I have written it primarily to honor my daughter Laura for the gift she is in my life.

Young women in our culture today are searching for strong role models, for guiding lights to go before them and show them the way. They are searching for other women who will speak the truth in love and share the sacredness of their own lives before God. They need to hear what has worked well and what has not worked well. They are asking those of us who are older to say what it means to be a woman who knows, loves, and believes in the God who made us.

While many young women have found good models within their own families, churches, communities, and schools, others are still searching. These women, along with the rest of us, need to be reminded of the courageous women who have gone before them in their journeys of faith.

The most encouraging resources for us to turn to are the women whose lives emerge from Scripture. The Bible is filled with "a cloud of witnesses," a whole host of strong women whose sacred voices span its pages, whose lives were precious in the sight of God.

I first met these women of the Bible years ago, and in recent years have become reacquainted with their stories. Each of these women have complex and multifaceted personalities, and while I could have approached their lives from any number of directions, I chose to single out a particular life theme that strengthened my own walk with God. These women have touched my life in remarkable ways, and it is the "light" from their lives that I want to pass on. I hope what I have written here will be helpful to you as well.

These women of strength struggled with overcoming real problems. They encountered many of the same kinds of struggles you and I face. All of them faced obstacles and what appeared to be impossible odds. Most of them made courageous and difficult choices. Most of them relied on God. None of them, not one, escaped God's love.

While a few of them chose poorly, their lives teach us to choose differently. Most of the women I've included in this book had their lives transformed by the powerful and loving hand of God. They are inspiring women to know.

God recorded their names in history and called them—through the voice of Isaiah—in the same way he calls us:

> "Fear not, for I have redeemed you;
> I have summoned you by name;
>   you are mine.
> When you pass through the waters,
>   I will be with you;
> and when you pass through the rivers,
>   they will not sweep over you.
> When you walk through the fire, you
>   will not be burned; the flames will
>   not set you ablaze.
> For I am the LORD, your God."
>   (Isa. 43:1–3)

God knows our names and cares about our circumstances because we are his.

It's important to remember that a woman's name in the Bible meant more than a mere label. Her name revealed her identity, her character, her whole being. So when God called the names of these women to come to him, he called every part of them, heart and soul and mind and strength. He called these women to come to him out of the circumstances of their lives, to depend on him, to believe in him, and to trust that he cared about them and would provide all they needed by his own hand.

As the lives of these women shine through the centuries of time to illuminate our paths, they help guide us through our own uncertainties, fears, and failures into the arms of the one who knows and loves us best.

Over the years, both in and out of the classroom, I have met many wonderful young women. I have been privileged to know many who are searching for what really matters in life. They want to know if God knows their names, if he cares. They want to know if they, like these women of the past, have found his favor and if God has taken the time to notice them. My answer to all of their concerns is yes.

God knows your name and mine. He has noticed us and we have found his favor. Just as he cared about Ruth, Esther, and Jochebed, he cares about us. Just as Jesus called Mary Magdalene's name in the garden, he calls ours. Just as the angel Gabriel announced good news to Mary, he announces to us, "Greetings, you who are highly favored! The Lord is with you" (Luke 1:28).

I hope you will allow these women who walked so intimately with God to impact your life. I hope you will open your heart and mind and truly hear what they have to say, finding that, along with them, you have been caught in a higher love.

Each chapter included in this book examines a theme reflected in the life of a woman in the Bible. Following each chapter, I have included a prayer, a series of questions to consider for journal entries or group discussion, and finally, a list of Scriptures to read to further explore the lives of these remarkable women.

Mary

Trust

*"I am the Lord's servant," Mary
answered. "May it be to me as
you have said." (Luke 1:38)*

*"Greetings, you who are highly
favored! The Lord is with you."
(v. 28)*

I have come to love the name Mary. I love
the name mainly because it is a name that rings of gladness. Mary was the name of the mother of Jesus. God
chose this young woman to be the mother of his one and
only Son. What an honor! What a blessing! God noticed
her, and her reputation lives on today as the epitome of
what it means for a mother to trust God. Her name lives
on today because of the way she responded in faith to
God's will in her life.

Before God revealed to Mary her unique place in the
world, she was on a different track altogether. She was in
the middle of building what she believed would be the
good life with her fiancé, Joseph. Like the rest of us, she
was busy making her own plans. As quite a young
woman, Mary was called to give it all before she really
even got started. God called her to let go of her own
plans and to enter into his will.

Mary's story opens quietly in Scripture as a Jewish
teenager engaged to a carpenter. She was embarking on

5

one of life's major adventures: her marriage. No doubt she and Joseph, like other young couples, had discussed their wedding plans and dreamed about the rest of their lives together as husband and wife.

Then suddenly, on an ordinary day, God sent an unmistakable message to Mary. Joseph wasn't even present. God sent the angel Gabriel straight to Mary with startling news. It was a disturbing surprise, to say the least, in the middle of all the plans she was making with Joseph. God spoke directly to her ears and to her heart while she listened intently to every single word.

The angel Gabriel announced the will of God for Mary's life. He told her that she would conceive a son, that his name would be Jesus, and that he would be great. Mary was stunned at first. She felt confused and afraid as she focused on the very question that any virgin would have asked, "How can I have a baby without a husband?" In other words, "I hear what you're saying, Gabriel, but this isn't making any sense. This is a physical impossibility." Mary was saying, "No, Gabriel, this can't be."

And the angel's answer? "This is God's work in you, Mary. Nothing is impossible with God" (Luke 1:37 paraphrase). *Oh*, she thought, *God's work*. Then Gabriel, to encourage Mary and to reveal God's power, told her about another woman in whose life God was working. He told her that her childless cousin Elizabeth, who was too old to have a baby, was already in her sixth month (v. 36). Suddenly, Mary was jolted out of her own plans, not just for the day, but for the rest of her life. She awakened to the reality that God had something quite different in mind for her and that he could—and would—accomplish his plans through her.

What was Mary's next response? Although I imagine Mary needed some additional time to process these startling words from God, I'm amazed at her immediate response of faith: "I am the Lord's servant. May it be to me as you have said" (v. 38). In essence she said to Gabriel, "I live to do God's will." She was quite a mature spiritual woman for her age. She knew where to pin her real hopes and dreams. There was no argument, no complaining, no "But what will the neighbors say?" or "How will Joseph take the news?"

And I imagine the neighbors had plenty to say, not just then, but for a long time afterward. Mary's news gave Joseph so much to think about that he considered breaking their engagement. But rather than considering her reputation with her neighbors or her relationship with Joseph, the first thing Mary considered was her relationship with God. Rather than considering the whole revelation an absurd impossibility, Mary believed God.

The thing that stands out in Mary's story is her faith in God's will for her life. Mary trusted God from the very start of things, and as the mother of God's only Son, she would be called on to keep that faith over and over again.

Mary didn't hang her head down and wallow in the worries of her circumstances. She didn't act in fear of what Joseph would think about her or what others might say. Mary believed that somehow God would take care of those matters, and even more important, she believed that what God had said would happen! His work would be done. Surely she didn't have a complete understanding of things. I'm certain that she had more than a few questions along the way, but she knew who to trust.

After God's revelation to her, Mary showed an even deeper faith in God, as she expressed her gratitude to him before Jesus was even born. She quickly turned to an older, wiser woman of God who, without question, would understand and be able to share in her joy. She remembered her cousin Elizabeth and poured out her faith and her gratitude as she sang the song of her heart:

"Praise God from all that is within me.
God has noticed me.
He has shown his great mercy to me and
to all of those who come after me.
See what a great thing he has done
for me,
and look how he has kept his promise to
bless forever all who have come after
Abraham." (vv. 46–55 paraphrase).

Mary had kept God's Word in her heart for many years. She knew his promises throughout her family history. And here she was, an ordinary young woman, the one chosen by God to help accomplish his purpose in the world. Of course, Mary sang a song of joy.

Even though angels sang on the day Mary's baby boy was born, the world didn't really know him. As her son grew, Mary did all the things for Jesus that good mothers do. She presented him in the temple according to the law and custom. She took Jesus to the synagogue and the special feast days. She taught him God's Word. She did everything she knew to do as a young Jewish mother to nurture, support, and encourage her son. In the process she tried to understand this son of hers, but she didn't—not really, not until the end. Mary was called on over and over again during the entire course of her son's life to put her faith in God. She was reminded that this was God's work.

Jesus, without question, challenged and fostered Mary's faith the most. Many believe he was not the only son Mary had, but he was the son she had to let go of time and again. This was the son whose life she saved when he received a death threat before he was two years old, forcing Joseph and her to leave the country. And this was the son she couldn't save later on in the full flush of his early manhood. In the end, he traded places with his mother and saved her instead.

This was the son who amazed her in the temple when he was only twelve years old. He was preparing for a ministry that would change the world. As she listened to Jesus, she must have remembered the voice of Gabriel saying, "This is God's work, Mary."

This was the son whose words Mary learned to trust. When he spoke, others listened—even during a socially embarrassing incident at a small-town wedding feast they were attending in Cana. When the bridegroom ran out of wine, Mary boldly told the servants, "Do whatever my son tells you to do" (John 2:5 paraphrase).

This was the son whose miraculous acts of grace, witnessed all over the country of Palestine, reached Mary's proud ears. And this was the son whose brutal rejection by the religious establishment pierced her heart. This was the son lifted high on a Roman cross, blood spilling from his body. This was the son whose last words of love rang in her ears until her dying breath as she heard him say to his dearest friend on earth, "Take care of my mother" (19:26–27 paraphrase). Did she question then if his death, too, was God's work?

As she helplessly stood by and watched Jesus die an agonizing and humiliating death on a cross, perhaps she hopelessly asked along with all the others, "What does it all mean?" Perhaps she was tempted to think, *Did I really hear the voice of God before his birth or was it my imagination?* And after her son's death, his burial, and his resurrection, a voice inside reminded her again, "Yes, Mary, this too is God's work."

Why did God choose Mary from among all the women of her day and age to bear his only Son, Jesus? She wasn't chosen because she had developed the art of motherhood perfectly or because of her astute understanding of twelve-year-old boys or of young men embarking on their chosen careers. In fact, over and over we read of Mary's misunderstanding of and astonishment at her son. I believe Mary was chosen because she remained resolutely focused on God's will for her life.

Why was Mary chosen? Mary answers the question best in her own words. At the very beginning of her story, she described herself to the angel Gabriel as "the handmaid of the Lord" (Luke 1:38 KJV). She spoke of God's will as the most important thing in her life. No doubt she had to contend with nosy neighbors who wanted to know how and why she got pregnant before she was married. No doubt she had to deal with those who wanted to bring her down in disgrace and humiliation. No doubt Joseph's initial feelings of shame and disgrace concerned her.

It's interesting to note, though, that those stories are all forgotten. They aren't even a part of recorded history, even though the probability of their occurring is high. We don't remember Mary's loss of reputation or the social embarrassment. We remember she was given a reputation above all women of the world by God himself as the mother of his one and only Son, Jesus. We remember that Mary was as faithful to God as she knew how to be.

Do you think Mary understood the circumstances she was placed in? Do you think she understood the mission of her son Jesus while he lived? I doubt it. But she did trust in God. And with the kind of faith that accepts God's Word for what it is, Mary lived to see miracles happen. Mary was willing, even though she didn't fully

understand. She believed that God himself would accomplish the work in her that he gave her to do. She
counted her circumstances as nothing. She counted God
as everything.

How do you respond when God interrupts your plans
with his plans? When you hear the joyful news of God
himself, what is your response? Do you pass through your
own shock, confusion, and disbelief into a grateful faith?
Like Mary, do you sing your own Magnificat before God?
Like Mary, do you live to do God's will?

Today, God still sends messages for our ears alone that
can be both disturbing and wonderful at the same time,
occurring right in the middle of our life plans. Today, God
still calls us at surprising and unexpected times to accomplish his work in the world. His messages have a way of
suddenly turning our lives upside down, and, like Mary,
we can get caught a little off-guard at first, stunned with
the news before the gratitude sets in. What may appear
for a few moments to be our whole undoing can turn out
to be the greatest blessing we have ever experienced.

One of the ways the world is blessed occurs when
we are called to be mothers. We are changed by the
lives of the sons and daughters we are privileged to bring
into this world. Miracles happen. The whole world
changes because of the lives that we bear, holy lives
(Gen. 1:26–28) given by God himself. And like Mary,
our whole work is to trust God when our plans are interrupted. Our whole work is to trust God when we are
called to be mothers. Once we do trust, the new adventure of our lives begins.

Today, God is still sending his image-bearing sons
and daughters to women as newborn babies to accomplish his work.

In the process of giving birth to our children, of rear-
ing, teaching, and accepting them for who they are, and

seeing them through until the very end, we are called to do one thing and one thing only: to remain faithful to the one who has sent them to us and changed our lives and all the world.

Prayer

I praise your name, O God, that you have called me to be a mother in your world.

I praise your name for the sons and daughters that I have been/will be privileged to bear.

I praise your name, O God, for the wonder of the work that you call me to do in this world and for the wonder of the work that you call my sons and my daughters to do.

When my plans are interrupted, may I gratefully give my will to you and trust your will for me.

Journal Entries

1. When have your important plans been interrupted by God?
2. What was your response?

Scripture References

Matthew 1:16–25; 13:55; Luke 1:26–56; 2:41–50; Acts 1:14; John 2:1–11; John 19:25

Sarah

A Promise Is a Promise

*"Is anything too hard for the
LORD?" (Gen. 18:14)*

Well over thirty years ago, a friend of mine
tearfully and anxiously disclosed a confidence to me over
the telephone. Then at the end of the conversation, she
asked me not to tell anyone her secret. I didn't. And I
haven't. I'm sure she doesn't even know that I've kept
her confidence all these years, but for whatever it's
worth, I'm glad I did it. I kept a promise. I kept a promise
to a principle, but more than that—I kept a promise to a
person.

In more recent history, I went to see a delightful
movie entitled *It Could Happen to You*, starring Nicholas
Cage and Bridget Fonda. The storyline follows a New
York cop who inadvertently misplaced his wallet and
didn't have the change to pay a struggling, near penniless
waitress for a cup of coffee. With a look of chagrin he
pulled out a lottery ticket from his pocket, held it before
her, and laughingly said that if he won, he would give
her half his winnings. The rest of the story tells about his
actual winning of the lottery and his insistence, against
his wife's loud protests, to give the waitress what he said
he would. After all, as he kept repeating, "A promise is a
promise."

Was that an absurd thing he did? Under the circumstances, did he have to follow through with his promise?

13

He unexpectedly won all that money, and he certainly was under no legal obligation to give that waitress any of his winnings. His value system said something different. His value system said his word was as good as gold or better than gold. He willingly took a huge financial loss to keep his word to the waitress. He valued the principle of promise-keeping, and he valued the person he made the promise to.

In real life we often find ourselves in situations or relationships where other people don't value promise-keeping. They don't have the same value system, pleading "temporary forgetfulness." Have you ever had someone in your life go back on a promise? Perhaps it was someone you had really counted on, and when the going got rough, he withdrew his support. Not a pleasant experience at all! That's life though. It happens. Others fail to keep their promises to us, and we're left in the lurch at critical times in our lives.

Here's another question for you: Are you a promise-keeper or a promise-breaker? If we're truly honest with ourselves, we may have to admit that we find ourselves in both roles at one time or another in the course of our well-intentioned lives. At the beginning of this chapter, I related a story about a time I kept a promise. While I think of myself as a promise-keeper, I must confess that I've come up short at times, falling down on my part of the bargain. I'm trying to pay closer attention to the promises I make in my life.

Most of us admire a promise-keeper because we know that's a person we can count on. God is that kind of friend. He keeps his promises to us. Amazingly, he keeps a covenant, even when we don't.

When things appeared to be totally impossible, God kept a covenant with a woman in her nineties whose

them. Sarah laughed at the promise. After all those years of hearing about God's promise to Abraham that he would be a great nation and that a son would come through her, Sarah could not believe that it was really going to happen. She had given up and lost hope.

She responded to God's personal promise in the same way we do at times. "This can't be," we say. We think we're too old or too tired or too weak or too something else. What we may mean is that we're too human. What we probably mean is that in our own strength we can't accomplish it.

If, in my humanness, I cannot fathom the promises of God to me or don't know how in the world he will accomplish them, I can draw the wrong conclusion, considering his promise to be impossible. That's the whole point! God calls us to believe that he can accomplish what is impossible for us. God accomplishes his marvelous, miraculous promises through feeble men and women on this earth, like Abraham and Sarah, and like you and me.

We moan and groan when our faith falters, and we refuse to hear the promises of God in our own lives. Do we believe the promise of God that Paul writes in Romans 8 that nothing in the heavens above or in the earth below can separate us from the love of God? Do we hear his promise from Hebrews 13, "I will never leave you"? Do we believe that God meant that he continues to love us and refuses to leave us when our hearts are broken—when our marriages fail, or when our children go away to college, or when our mothers have to leave the only home they've ever known to live in a personal care facility, or when our best friends walk out the door, or when our company decides to cut back and we're the ones they're letting go.

There are a thousand other ways that life hands us
the pink slip of rejection and abandonment. We wake up
in the night alone with the question, "Do I believe?"
Right now, in today's set of circumstances, do we believe
God? We hem and haw and struggle and complain, "But
I didn't expect this." Or like Sarah we cry, "I'm too old,
too tired, too weak."

Can we hear God saying Sarah's name, but not ours?
Does God's promise to Sarah make sense, but his promise
to us doesn't? Is it OK for Sarah to wait on God's special
delivery for twenty-five years, but it's not OK for us to
wait a day or a year or longer? What is it about people
whose lives were recorded in the Bible that makes us
believe their relationships with God were real and ours
aren't, or that makes us believe that somehow God loved
them but he doesn't care about us? That's the primary
reason their lives are on record: to help us in our unbe-
lief. If God could do this impossible thing for Sarah at
the age of ninety, then what can or what will he do for
you and me?

Listen for a moment to God's response to Sarah when
she struggled with belief. Listen to what he said when she
more or less laughed in the face of his promise. "Is anything too hard for the LORD?" (Gen. 18:14).

And what about you and me? Do we believe in the
promises of God at a distance, but not when they get too
close and personal? What is it in your personal life that
has caused you to say, "God, this is too hard even for you.
There is no way you can deliver on this one"? Again, the
only question for you to answer is, "Do I believe?" It all
comes down to that.

God has a plan. He has given us life and made a
promise: "I can deliver. I can deliver you out of, or
through, the hardest circumstance that you can imagine.

18

Just watch me." The only way I know for our faith to
grow is for us to believe God and watch him do his work.

Where are you in your life today? Is God ready to
deliver on a promise to you? Which one is it? What circumstance are you in that is greater than his promise?

At the ripe old age of ninety, the surprise of Sarah's
life was the moment she heard the words, "Sarah, you're
going to have a son." She probably felt a lot like Moses
when God called him to go back to Egypt and deliver the
Israelites from the bondage of Pharoah. "Well, I don't
think so, God. Not right now." She probably felt a lot
like Mary when Gabriel announced that she would have
the Son of God and she said, "How can this be?" Mary
couldn't figure it out anymore than Sarah could. It was
just too incredible. It defied all the laws of logic and of
culture. "How can it possibly happen now to me?"

Then we read these remarkable words about the very
next year, the very next chapter of Sarah's life. "Now the
LORD was gracious to Sarah as he had said, and the LORD
did for Sarah what he had promised. Sarah became pregnant and bore a son to Abraham in his old age, at the
very time God had promised him" (21:1–2). Sarah had a
baby when she was ninety! God delivered right on time
with his promise.

In the face of our weak faith, in the shallows of our
disbelief, God says to us, "Let me show you how it's done.
A promise is a promise. Whether your belief is shaky or
not, I'll keep my end of the bargain. If you watch me
long enough, then maybe you'll catch on."

Sarah caught on. She laughed when her baby boy was
born, but it wasn't a laughter that said to God, "I don't
believe you." It was a laughter of faith that said, "I can't
believe what you just did for me. This is incredible. It's so
incredible that it could only have come from you. I never

could have accomplished it on my own. Here's the evidence right here laying in my arms, a son."

The name *Isaac* means "laughter." What a wonderful name for a son whose parents laughed, at first because they thought they wouldn't have a son, and who laughed in the end because they did.

God keeps his promises. When things appeared impossible, God kept a covenant with a husband and his wife who were in their nineties. God still works that way. He sends reminder after reminder from the past and in the present. "Is anything too hard for the Lord?"

While it may be hard for us to keep promises at times, it isn't hard for God. God keeps his promises, and he calls us to keep the promises we make because promise-keeping blesses. A promise is a promise. God is the great promise-keeper of all time. He'll never bail out on us, and he'll help us not to bail out on each other. He'll remind us of what it means to keep promises and of the untold blessings in store for those who do.

After Isaac was born, Sarah called for those around her and for all the rest of us down through the ages to join in the laughter of belief. We are still reaping the benefits of God keeping his promise to Sarah.

With the miraculous birth of Isaac by the power of God came the beginning of great and good things: the Jewish nation, the coming of the Messiah, numerous descendants. Isaac was the beginning of all those who would follow after and, like his mother Sarah, enter into the joy of believing that nothing is too hard for God to accomplish. The God who makes promises keeps them.

Prayer

Help me, O God, to believe in your promises to me.

When I am up against what appears to me to be impossible odds, help me to know that nothing is impossible for you.

When I've waited for a long time or grown tired, help me still to believe.

Thank you, O God, that you are faithful to keep your promises.

Journal Entries

1. When have you experienced disbelief concerning a promise of God?

2. What was the promise?

3. What blocked your belief?

4. When have you experienced belief in a particular promise of God?

5. Is there anything in your life today that you believe may be too hard for God to accomplish?

Scripture References

Genesis 11:29–31; 12:1–9; 15:1–6; 17; 18:1–15; 21:1–7; 23; 25:10; 49:31; Romans 4:19; Hebrews 11:11–12

Letting Go

*"For this son of mine was dead
and is alive again; he was lost
and is found." (Luke 15:24)*

Imagine the day when your son grows up and becomes a young man. He's in the prime of his youth, and you have all these hopes and dreams for who he'll become and what he'll do with his life; then one day he walks in the door at the end of the day and says to his father in a determined voice, "Give me my inheritance, now." Very soon on a day after that, he packs up everything he owns and leaves home. He goes as far away as he possibly can, and the only news that comes home is bad news. Your son that you love better than your own life is throwing away every dime of his inheritance on sex, drinking, and drugs. What does a mother do when she wakes up to this kind of a nightmare?

Although the parable of the prodigal son emphasizes the love of the father, I want to take an imaginary look at who his mother might have been. This is the story of a woman who is given no name by the storyteller. She isn't even mentioned in the story, though both her husband and her two sons are. Did she die of heartache? Is that why she isn't mentioned? Or did she live to see the day when things made sense again? Even though the father and sons are the ones we usually focus on, because they are the ones named and she isn't, let's imagine, for the

23

sake of our own homes, that she was there in the house when her young son left home and she had to let him go.

What was her home like? Well, we know that she had a lovely home with lovely things and plenty of servants to get things done. She was married to a man who apparently had "done well." They had two sons. And even though things went haywire for a while, the day did come when things made sense again in this family, but not in the old way. It made sense in a brand-new way.

As in most homes, there was some kind of unrest in this home as well. It influenced the younger son to ask for his share of his father's inheritance and to walk away from the family. It's interesting to imagine what might have caused his leaving. But again that's a detail the storyteller doesn't directly reveal to us. It wasn't the focus of the story.

We can be certain of this observation. The unrest in this home existed inside the son himself. He experienced some primal cry to be loved in a way that he had never known. There was a cry in his soul that he could not speak about, or even name, and to solve the pain he had to experience as many of the world's answers as he could before he found the only answer that worked.

The mother had to let her son go. In letting him go, she had a number of choices. She could write him off. She could rage against the injustice of it all. She could grieve his leaving. And she may have done all of these and much, much more. Another possibility is that she could have dropped to her knees and prayed for his return, lifting her son through prayer into the loving arms of the Father and trusting that all would be well. I have a feeling she made her way through all the stages of grief, anger, and hurt because, eventually, her son came home, and things were never the same again. I imagine the process was difficult.

What did the process of letting go look like for this mother? Did she go through the process of blaming herself for her son's leaving? Did she ask these familiar questions, "Where did I go wrong?" and "What could I have done differently?" Worrying was not going to change the fact that her son was gone. At this point, the most effective and most healing thing she could have done for herself, her family, and her son was to fall down on her knees and pray.

This mother's younger son made a geographical move to try to solve things. He went away to a far place, and he went wild! While his mother and father were grieving over his loss and missing his presence at home every day, he was going hog-wild.

After he spent every dime he had on the wildest kind of living he could imagine, he found out that no one wanted to have anything to do with him. What a sobering experience! He didn't even have money for food. His feelings of worthlessness grew with every passing day. He experienced deprivation on every hand. No food. No friends. No decent, respectable job. Lost. Alone. Scared.

Then a critical thing happened. The writer tells us that "he came to his senses" (Luke 15:17). This means he faced reality; he saw things for what they really were, and he saw himself for who he really was: a sinner before God. He made the discovery of all discoveries that, like the rest of us, he had sinned against his family and against God. He could see his sins and name them. There was no room to place the blame on anybody else's head. He must have asked himself a thousand times, "Why under God's heaven did I run away from all the love I had?"

The only place left to go now was home. And oddly enough, now, that was the only place he wanted to go.

Ever lost a son? Ever had to let a son go far enough away so that he could find his way back home, or so he

could find something you couldn't give him? Ever had to
let a son go so far away from home that you couldn't protect him anymore? Ever had to let a son go far enough
away from home so that he could find the only thing that
matters in all the world is the love of God?

Often we find the love of God when we are farthest
from home, bingeing on everything the world says will
bring us what we need. Often we find love when we are
lost, alone, and deprived—when we need it most.

Was the love of God real inside this mother? It must
have been. It's the only way that she could have let him
go. Mothers have to let sons (and daughters) go so that
they can find their way home to the love of God. While
sons are away, mothers are called to trust God with all
their heart, soul, and strength. They are called to pray
long into the night.

The woman in this story isn't given a name because
she wears every mother's name. She is every God-
fearing mother who goes the distance with her child so
that when she can't change the circumstance of a lost
son—alone in wild living—she prays and trusts in the
God who can. What matters in the story is what happened in her home. What matters is her son. Her son
came home! He did find his way back. He "was dead and
is alive again; he was lost and is found" (v. 32). Things
did make sense again.

There was another mother, named Mary, who had to
let her son go too. She was forced, in the midst of her
own pain, disgrace, and confusion, to trust that in the
Father's open arms of love, all would be well in the end.
And so it was. And so it is.

Prayer

O God, as a mother, I am grateful to you for my children you sent me.

It is my desire to love, protect, and guide them.

It is hard when I am called to let go.

When I am in that place, show me the way to you, O God.

Help me to turn to you and to trust you with all my heart, soul, mind, and strength.

Help me to place my children that I love better than life itself into your open arms of love, knowing that you care for them and love them in a way far better than I could ever imagine.

Journal Entries

1. As a mother have you had to let go of a child?

2. What were the circumstances?

3. What were the results?

4. How did you go through the process? What helped? What didn't help?

5. What message would you pass on to other mothers who may be experiencing the same harsh reality?

Scripture Reference

Luke 15:11–32

Turning It Over

*Eli answered, "Go in peace, and
may the God of Israel grant
you what you have asked of
him."... Then she went her
way and ate something, and her
face was no longer downcast.
(1 Sam. 1:17–18)*

How long does a woman wait for the thing
she prays for? How much suffering does a woman endure
until she receives from God's own hand the thing that is
missing in her life? How does a woman know, in the
midst of her tears and grief, what to do? How does a
woman give back to God the thing that she wants most
in all the world?

It is human to need meaning and purpose. Women
throughout the centuries have searched for and found
meaning in their lives in different ways. Some have
found it through marriage; some in relationships with
friends; some through their work; some through painting,
writing, or dance; some through service to others; and
some through having children.

Hannah was a woman who desperately needed meaning in her life. More than anything else in all the world,
she wanted a son.

During the time that Hannah lived it was important
for women to have children, especially sons. One obvious

reason was so the family could have an adequate source of physical labor to help with the work. Ideally, the number of sons for an Israelite family to strive for was seven (Ruth 4:15). It hasn't been that many years since families in our own society needed sons for similar reasons. In an agricultural society where families were dependent on the land, more sons were needed to cultivate and produce more food.

An even more important reason to have a son during Hannah's lifetime was to pass on the family name. In fact, in Israel there was no greater tragedy than for a family name to die out and no greater honor than for a family name to live on. Without a son to carry on the name, there was no way for the family to live on in this sense of the term.

Another reason for a woman to have a son during the time in which Hannah lived was that many believed then, as many believe today, that children are a blessing from God.

What if you, like Hannah, wanted more than anything else in the whole world to have a child and you could not. What would you do? To what lengths would you go? How would you respond when others with children were unkind? Can you imagine the fears and the uncertainties that this circumstance of childlessness must have caused for her?

No one really understood the depth of Hannah's pain. Her husband Elkanah tried to help. He deeply loved Hannah. He cared about her childlessness. He was tender and kind and attentive. He listened to her and tried to comfort her in her sadness, but he had no way of really understanding her situation. He asked, "Hannah, why are you weeping? . . . Don't I mean more to you than ten sons?" (1 Sam. 1:8). He hoped that his loving presence in her life could make up for the loss of sons, but it couldn't.

Even at worship, as they offered a sacrifice, Elkanah tried to be especially attentive to Hannah by giving her a double portion of the meat sacrificed, but in his desire to help he may have actually made things worse.

While he showed such concern for Hannah, his other wife, Peninnah, who had many sons and daughters, watched and waited to pay Hannah back in the cruelest and most hurtful of ways. She deliberately hurled insults at Hannah because she had children and Hannah did not. Out of her selfishness, jealously, and misunderstanding of the depth of Hannah's pain, she said such mean-spirited and thoughtless things that she provoked Hannah to tears.

At worship, of all places, as Hannah watched the children run and play and sing and dance, Hannah received reminder after reminder about her own childlessness by someone who had no compassion for her circumstance. Eventually, Hannah became so despondent that she refused to eat.

This other woman who was so focused on competing with Hannah could have freely given out of a wealth of blessings—husband, home, and children—but she refused. This malicious taunting went on year in and year out, as the anger, hurt, and disappointment built inside Hannah's heart.

One day Hannah couldn't take it anymore. The worshipers at Shiloh had finished eating and drinking as Hannah stood up with tears streaming down her tormented face, and she began silently to pray to God. That was Hannah's turning point. This wasn't the first prayer Hannah had prayed. She had gone with the others to the house of the Lord year after year to pray. This prayer was a longer prayer, a different prayer.

31

Hannah shifted the focus in this prayer. Somehow she turned her circumstance over to God. She made a major shift from self to God. I can guess, but I don't really know Hannah's real motivation in wanting a son so desperately. I just know that one day Hannah had taken all she could take. She was on her last leg as she poured out her heart and soul to God. She made a bargain with God, "If you will give me a son, then I'll give him back to you" (see v. 11). Do you hear the emphasis in that prayer?

We need meaning in our lives as women, and we go about that process in different ways trying to remove the emptiness and fill up our lives with what we believe we need most. Sometimes the process involves our getting to the point where we put first things first. As Hannah engaged the process of finding meaning, she cried. She suffered rejection and embarrassment and humiliation, which was part of the necessary process to bring her to the place where she needed to be.

When we are in a miserable circumstance, and no one around seems to really understand—not even the people who love us most—God does, and things begin to change when we go to him. Miracles happen. Hannah turned to God with a different kind of prayer, and things changed.

Even God's priest, Eli, misunderstood what was going on. He hurt Hannah before he was able to help her. Sitting by the doorpost of the temple, Eli watched Hannah stand up. He noticed that her lips kept moving for a long time, but no sound was coming out. No doubt he saw the anguish in her contorted face as he falsely accused her of being drunk. This man of God made a wrong assumption, and in the process, he added insult to an already injured woman. "Stop getting drunk, Hannah.

Get rid of your wine" (v. 14 paraphrase). In the face of such an unfair accusation, Hannah turned to Eli and revealed to him the truth of what was on her heart. "I have been pouring out my heart to God. I am deeply troubled and have been praying out of my great grief," she said (v. 15 paraphrase).

Then Eli did what he needed to do. He did what Hannah needed most. He responded with compassion, understanding, and support. He held up her arms and joined her in prayer for the thing she wanted most from God: "Go in peace, and may the God of Israel grant you what you have asked of him" (v. 17).

From that day forward, Hannah believed that God would eventually answer her prayer and give her a son. She turned it over. She let go of the problem. Rather than grieving her loss any longer, Hannah believed her request would be answered. She left the temple, ate something, and came out of her depression. Now it was in God's hands, not hers.

And God did do for Hannah the very thing that she asked of him. God remembered Hannah and she gave birth to a son named Samuel, whose name means "asked of the Lord." When Samuel was born, the son she held most dear in all the world, Hannah was willing to give him back to God. "He's yours now for his whole life" (v. 27 paraphrase). Hannah wasn't bitter or fearful or sad. She prayed:

> My heart rejoices in the Lord.
> He has delivered me.
> He is my strength. He is my Rock.
> There is no one holy like the Lord.
> (2:1–2 paraphrase).

Often we pray for a day and feel as though we have spent an eternity praying over something dear to our hearts. A day is a long time, but our timetable is not God's timetable. As a woman of prayer, Hannah prayed for years. She desired a son more than anything in the world. She made a vow to God to dedicate this son to him, and she lived to see the desire of her heart granted by God.

When Samuel was old enough, Hannah brought him to the temple to live with Eli the priest and serve the Lord there. Samuel grew spiritually and became the prophet who anointed the first king of Israel, King Saul. Samuel also became the prophet who anointed David as king of Israel. He served the Lord all his days.

Hannah changed her perspective when she was able to pray, "If you will give me a son, I will give him back to you." Perhaps Hannah had hoped for a son for mixed reasons. Perhaps she wanted a son to achieve social acceptance or her husband's acceptance or acceptance of herself. Perhaps this was the turning point for this woman of God, when she could let go of selfish motives and be willing to give her son back to God. This was the prayer that she "kept on praying" until the priest Eli noticed her.

Hannah got to the point of asking for a son for selfless reasons to bless others. This is the place in prayer that we can all strive for. When our deepest desire is found in blessing others through what we receive from God, that is when we find true meaning in our lives. When we can take the focus off of self and give the gifts God has given us for the sheer joy of giving them, without any expectation, that is when we are most alive.

May God in his own time and in his own way give you the desires of your heart.

Prayer

O God, there are so many things I want in my life.

There are so many things that I think would make my days brighter.

You know exactly what those things are.

May my heart's greatest desire be to offer up to you what you so freely and so generously give to me.

Help me, in asking for those things, to depend on you.

Journal Entries

1. What is it today that you don't have that you want more than anything else in all the world?

2. Is there someone in your life who understands?

3. Is there someone in your life who does not understand? How does the misunderstanding affect you?

4. Have you offered your heart's desire to God in prayer?

5. Are you willing to give back to him the very thing that you want most in life and let him have his way?

Scripture References

1 Samuel 1–2; Luke 1:46; Ruth 4:15

Jochebed

The Power of Love

*So the woman took the baby and
nursed him. When the child grew
older, she took him to Pharaoh's
daughter and he became her son.
(Exod. 2:9–10)*

The power of love is an amazing thing. It is
amazing to see what quiet women of strength who hold
that kind of power can accomplish.

I had an aunt who held the power of love. Although
she didn't have a formal high school education, she loved
to read poetry and play her guitar, and she knew more
than most about how to live in the world.

She and her husband were both hard workers. They
lived in the country and knew very little of life's com-
forts. They didn't have any children of their own,
although they cared for my father during the Depression
when he came to live with them as a young teenager. My
Uncle Tom was a truck farmer who owned a market in
downtown Memphis along Front Street on the banks of
the Mississippi River. He raised every conceivable kind of
fruit and vegetable in his garden, and on occasion he and
my aunt worked side by side in the fields. My Aunt Edna,
however, spent most of her time taking care of her own
chores: canning fruits and vegetables, milking the cows,
collecting the eggs, and selling them to nearby neighbors.
Their work days began at 4:00 A.M.

My father watched Aunt Edna carefully and learned from her. He watched her work hard without complaint. He went to church with her and eventually became a real student of the Bible himself. She loved him and, as a result, her love had a powerful effect on his entire life.

One of my favorite stories about this wonderfully strong woman is the story of my father and mother's move to Mississippi in 1948. When my dad had an opportunity to purchase a franchise for his own Ford dealership, he didn't have enough money to make the purchase, so my aunt and uncle loaned it to him. What he didn't know until years later, after he had repaid his debt, was that they had given him nearly all the money they had. That's a love story if I ever heard one. My aunt never counted the cost of her love or thought about the end results. She just had the power to love.

Without question the most inspiring woman that I can think of in this century is Mother Teresa. Born in 1910 in Yugoslavia, she came out of a place of total obscurity, quietly doing her works of charity and hope. Along the way she received the Nobel Peace Prize. Because of her great compassion and servant spirit, she has accomplished more than whole governments have been able to by helping the poorest of the poor, the hurting, and the dying in our world.

Mother Teresa saw the need. She didn't say, "Oh, this thing is too hard for me. I am only one woman." She didn't throw up her hands and say, "The odds are against me. This appears to be too impossible to accomplish." Instead, she concluded she was doing God's work in the world. He would find the way. Here was a world of men and women in need. How could she help them? What difference could she make in their lives? Rather than relying on presidents or preachers or kings or queens to

38

put it all into place, she relied in faith on the power of God to show her how to love.

Jochebed was another woman with the power to love. God showed her the way. God gave her the courage. While austere circumstances didn't deter my Aunt Edna and political agendas didn't deter Mother Teresa, neither did the oppression of the most powerful government in the world deter Jochebed from her course. The same compassion that moved my aunt and Mother Teresa forward moved Jochebed. Like Mother Teresa who had her eyes on helping one person at a time, and like my aunt who had her eyes on my father, Jochebed had her loving eyes on one child—her son, Moses.

Following the death of Joseph, the nation of Israel grew into the thousands. While the previous king had extended his favor to Israel, a new king came to the throne with little compassion or tolerance toward the growing number of Israelites living in Egypt. Rather than treating them as a favored people, he treated them as slaves, forcing them to build great cities and monuments. While the pharaoh tried to control the increasing number of Israelites living within his borders with oppression, the Israelites continued to multiply.

Pharaoh made another heinous attempt to control the growing population of the Hebrews. He commanded the Hebrew midwives, Shiphrah and Puah, to kill all the baby boys. What Pharaoh hadn't counted on was the fact that the midwives feared God more than they feared him. When Pharaoh confronted them and asked why they had let the baby boys live, they answered, "Hebrew women are not like Egyptian women; they are vigorous and give birth before the midwives arrive" (Exod. 1:19). Pharaoh then ordered all the Egyptians, "Every boy that is born you must throw into the Nile, but let every girl live" (v. 22). It was following this mandate that Jochebed gave birth to Moses.

Jochebed was a woman who, because of her love for her son, relied on God to help her find a way to save him. For three months she found a way to hide her child. How could a woman hide a little baby all that while so that none of the Egyptians knew about him? How is it that none of them heard him crying? Were there so many thousands of Israelites that the Egyptians couldn't keep track of all of them? Was he just one baby boy who slipped through the cracks when the Egyptians made their rounds looking for babies to destroy?

God never intended for Moses to be thrown into the river Nile and drowned. God had other plans for him and for the entire nation of Israel. Egyptians were teeming everywhere with hatred in their hearts for the Israelites, but God delivered Moses out of their hands.

When Jochebed couldn't hide her baby at home any longer, she made a decision to take a another huge risk. She made a papyrus basket just large enough for Moses and waterproofed it with tar and pitch so that it would float. She placed it among the tallest reeds along the river and asked her daughter, Miriam, to protect her baby brother. Along with the Hebrew midwives and her mother, Miriam was a quiet woman of strength who joined God's forces of love and faith against the death threat of the most powerful nation in the world.

God used Pharaoh's own daughter to rescue this baby boy. After coming one day to bathe in the river Nile, she walked along the bank with her attendants and saw the floating basket. When she sent a slave girl to bring it to her, she saw Moses crying, and her heart went out to this Hebrew baby. Miriam, who was standing nearby keeping watch, approached this Egyptian princess and asked her if she needed a Hebrew nurse for the baby. Her answer was yes. And Miriam brought the baby to his own mother, Jochebed. When he grew older, Jochebed took her baby to Pharaoh's daughter who gave him the name *Moses*, which means, "I drew him out of the water."

Jochebed took every action in the name of love. In the face of Pharaoh's threat to have all the baby boys drowned in the Nile, she relied on the power of God to help her. God used what was intended as a river of death as a river of life instead. Jochebed couldn't have known all the plans that God had in mind for her baby boy. She only knew that she loved him and that she would do whatever it took to keep him alive.

Jochebed loved powerfully. She risked everything to keep Moses alive. Little did she know that years later her baby boy would become the great leader of her people, and that God would call Moses to deliver the Hebrew people out of Egyptian slavery.

The power of love is limitless. God can use the love of one person to affect the lives of millions of people. Today we are still experiencing the effects of Jochebed's love for Moses: the deliverance of the Israelites, their return to their promised land of Canaan, and Moses as the great lawgiver who paved the way for freedom and deliverance through Christ's law of love. Moses was the son of a quiet woman of strength who knew how to love. She was a woman of such compassion and faith that she knew she could risk the oppression of an entire government because she had God on her side. That is powerful love.

Are you a woman with the power to love? Are you the kind of risk-taker who is willing to do whatever it takes for your baby boy or baby girl, or your friend, or your husband, or your mother, or your sister? Is your faith in the love of God that strong?

Love has a powerful ripple effect. Once the flow begins, it flows on and on from one heart to another heart, from one day to the next, from one year to the next, from one generation to the next, until millions of lives have been lifted out of oppression and slavery into life.

Last year a lovely friend of mine from Texas sent me a powerful book entitled *The Preaching Life* by Barbara Brown Taylor. One of her chapters which discusses the good Samaritan is simply entitled "Do Love." One of her conclusions about love is that we are called to just "do it." She writes that although there may be appropriate times to talk about love or try to understand it better or think about it, nothing takes the place of doing love. Just do love. The whole world changes as a result. My whole world changes when I just do love, and your whole world changes when you do.

Jochebed did love in her own house. She did love in her own backyard. She risked love in the face of oppression. She didn't think about it or discuss it or try to understand it better or take the time to count the cost. She loved her baby and, against the major political power in all the world, kept him safe for his great destiny in the hands of God.

Prayer

Help me, O God, when I'm tempted to think too hard about love or talk too long about it, to just love.

Remind me how much love you have lavished on me.

Remind me of how much those around me need love to live.

Help me not to count the cost of loving but, out of a grateful heart, let its power flow.

Journal Entries

1. Describe a person in your own life with the power to love.

2. Describe its effect in your life and the lives of others.

3. What oppression in your own life is causing you to count the cost of loving?

4. Is it worth it to keep loving no matter what?

5. Who do you turn to replenish your supply of love?

6. Does God's power to supply love ever run dry?

Scripture References

Exodus 1; 2; 6:20; Numbers 26:59

Contentment

*The LORD God commanded, . . .
"you must not eat from the tree
of the knowledge of good and evil,
for when you eat of it you will
surely die." . . . When the woman
saw that the fruit of the tree
was good for food and pleasing to
the eye, and also desirable for
gaining wisdom, she took some
and ate it. (Gen. 2:16–17; 3:6)*

I believe that within each of us there is a
remembrance of paradise, of where we have come from
and where we long to return. Do you have your own idea
of paradise? Take a few minutes to mentally describe
what it would look like and who would be present. If you
could have anything you wanted, be any place you
wanted to be, with whomever you wanted to be with,
and if you could chart your days exactly as you wanted
them to be, what would that look like for you? While
each of us may have different ideas concerning the loca-
tion of our paradise, most of us agree on these essentials:
beauty, peace, love, harmony, joy, and companionship.

My idea of paradise is simply home and family. I prefer a place sheltered in the woods with lush green lawns
and beautiful flower gardens, a place of quiet, rest,
comfort, beauty, and a shelter from the storms of life

where my family lives from day to day in gratitude for
and delight in each other. We delight in doing the work
that we are each called to do and applaud each other's
efforts. We move through our days and nights anchored
in the love and power of God, so we can make a mean-
ingful difference for good in the world we live in. We
gather at the table morning and evening, knowing that
nothing can disturb the love that moves among us,
knowing that we will stand by each other until the very
end—because of God.

I know a woman who literally had it all. She didn't
just dream of paradise. She lived there. Her name was
Eve, and from the time she entered the world, she had
everything she could possibly have dreamed of having—
only God dreamed it for her, and God made it all come
true. After creating Eve in his own spirit of love, God
welcomed her home to a garden called Eden. He nurtured every aspect of Eve's new life there, revealing to her
his perfect love.

Eve had the essentials of paradise. It was a place of
exquisite beauty. Eve could look in any direction and see
beauty all around from the sunlit, life-giving rivers that
flowed nearby, to exotic, colorful flowers that bloomed
day in and day out, to the fruitful trees that spotted the
hills and plains. She literally walked in breathtaking
beauty. She slept in it, ate from it, and drank from it
every single day of her life.

In her garden paradise, Eve had everything that she
needed. Nothing was missing. Every gardener that I know
has a vision of what's next, but in Eve's garden the vision
was complete. Fresh, pure water kept all of the plant life
as flowering and as fruitful as it could possibly be. No pol-
lution clouded the skies. The temperature of the sun was
perfect throughout the day, while gentle breezes cooled

the night air. God provided enough nourishing food for every living creature and enough variety that Eve could stroll the garden paths and pick and eat to her heart's content. The hand of God provided everything necessary.

But Eve wasn't alone. She had a husband, a soul mate, who became a man by the life-breath of God himself. They were designed for each other. He was a man who needed her companionship and help, a man who desired her and was committed to her. They had all the time in the world to walk and talk about the discoveries of each new day of their lives. All of the ingredients of a perfect love were present: commitment, equality, identity, respect, trust, and work.

Eve also had a job and a job description to go along with it. God told her exactly what to do, how to do it, and that she had help to do it. She worked beside Adam to care for all the living things in the garden, especially her husband. As she nurtured the plants, the flowers and the trees, the animals, and the man she loved, she was nurtured in the process. Sound ideal? It was. It was designed that way.

And God walked and talked with Eve. She didn't have to play guessing games with God. He told her everything that she needed to know about life in the garden. She was free to love and to enjoy all that God had provided for her. She knew everything she could do and everything she couldn't do in her garden paradise. God, the one who designed, planted, and placed Eve in the perfect setting said these words to her, "You are free to eat from any tree in the garden; but you must not eat from the tree of the knowledge of good and evil, for when you eat of it you will surely die" (Gen. 2:16–17).

I have wondered what Eve thought about the guidelines God gave her. Surely, no one could live in such perfection without thanking God for his good gifts? God provided for every single need that Eve had, even before she thought of what her needs were. But at some point she must have begun to think, "Maybe there's more. Just maybe I'm missing out on something." Is that so hard for us to imagine? What was it that caused Eve to shift the focus from God to self?

Eve listened to a lie. She listened to the master of lies. Once Satan had Eve's attention by suggesting that God was entirely too strict with his guidelines, he quickly turned God's truth into a full-fledged lie.

"Did God really say what you think he said, Eve dear? Well, Eve, God wasn't telling you the truth. The one who designed this place of beauty is holding out on you, Eve. You won't die if you eat of the tree in the middle of the garden. You'll live, and on top of that, you'll be as wise as God" (3:1, 4 paraphrase).

Eve looked at the tree in the middle of the garden through the eyes of the greatest liar of all time, and, as a result, the fruit of the tree appeared to be what it was not. It appeared to be good, ripe for the eating. Eve thought she would eat some of its good fruit and in the process gain enough wisdom to be as wise as God.

What was the driving force behind Eve's decision to finally eat the fruit of this tree? She couldn't really say that the devil made her do it. She had a choice in the matter. God had said one thing. Satan had said another. Maybe for the moment she was confused about God. After all, was God really God? Did God really mean what he said? How long could it take, anyway, to take a bite out of this lovely looking fruit? And what if Eve did gain wisdom? Surely God would understand.

God understood all right. It was Eve who didn't understand. God knew what he was talking about. Eve didn't. Was it hard for Eve to face her own pride? Did Eve suppose for a day that she could chart her own destiny apart from God's will for her? Do you suppose Eve concluded that maybe she knew what was best for her?

While Adam certainly had his part in this story, I want to focus on Eve's part. Look at the consequences of Eve's choice: fear, shame, pain, sorrow, disappointment, and death. A woman whose name meant "life" was a partner in bringing death, not just for herself, but for all living things, for all her sons and daughters, for all flowers and trees and animals, and for you and me. Look at all that Eve helped to set in motion.

Eve gained wisdom, all right. Her eyes were opened. Eve must have understood in an instant that it was not in her to direct her life. She was not the life-giver. Her choice had brought about the opposite of what she had thought it would. Her decision, along with Adam's, to sin against God's clear command had a rippling effect on the whole world. That is the nature of sin.

And what about the one who planned Eve's paradise in the first place? Death was not supposed to be part of the original plan. Amazingly, he wanted to bring Eve back to paradise one day. Eve's sin, as great as it was, did not extinguish the light and the love of God in her life.

Again, it would be her choice to remain faithful. And it would take a long while for God to put in place his plan of salvation. But after all, God was the one in charge. His plan was paradise, and Eve did not have the power to prevent God from accomplishing what he wanted to in the first place. In spite of her sin, God wanted Eve to know how much he loved her and that there was a way back home.

Paradise! Look at how great the love of God is. God gave Eve a lot of room for huge failure and sin in the paradise he provided, but when she chose sin, he didn't leave her there. God provided a way out. He put clothes on her back to protect her from the coming storms of life. He covered her with the blood of his own Son so that she could make a different choice. She could choose again to find her way back to God, to find her way back to paradise. She could choose life instead of death.

Even though Eve left God in a moment that changed the course of her life and all living things, God didn't—even for a single moment—leave Eve. Eve saw the light of God's presence in her life. She saw the goodness of God. But then she closed her eyes to him and to paradise. It was still there, but she closed her eyes. She closed her eyes to the beauty and peace and goodness that were all around her.

How in the world could evil have entered in? Eve let it. Eve chose it. The "mother of all living" chose it. She probably didn't mean to. She probably didn't mean to cause all the damage she caused. But then, neither do we. We don't foresee all the fallout from our selfish, prideful, and misinformed choices.

Do you have eyes to see the paradise that God has placed you in? Just as surely as God formed Eve, he formed us, too, in our mothers' wombs (Ps. 139:13). Just like Eve, God has created us in his image of love to care for all of his creation. He has placed us in a garden that we call earth and called us to be in relationship with him. He has given us the same freedom of choice that he gave our mother, Eve. The same powerful forces for good and for evil are within our garden. God has made his truth clear and accessible. What will we choose? Life with God? (Paradise?) Or death?

Are you listening to God's voice and his truth? Or, are you listening to the lies of another? Are you dissatisfied? Want more?

Do you see the provision God has made for you? Is there anything he has withheld from you, any need that he hasn't supplied? Have you asked him lately?

Because God has provided all that you need, take care of what he has given you. Tend your garden well. Do the work God designed for you to do: care for all the living things in your garden, especially the people who live there.

Choose carefully. Use your freedom wisely.

Watch out for snakes in your garden who want to steal away the bloom of love, the innocence of the day, the rivers of delight, the joy, the peace, the beauty, everything that is good and lovely and true. These snakes will send you careening headlong into an avalanche of pain and sorrow, disappointment and death.

When you do fall—and you will—don't give up! Reach up to the one who made you, to the one who wants you to live with him in paradise. Listen to his voice and believe him. Believe that he is who he says he is, that he loves you, that he wants you to have it all, that he knows what's best for you, and that he alone can make it happen. When you're tempted to taste the fruit of the wrong tree, remember the words of the psalmist, "Taste and see that the LORD is good" (34:8).

Prayer

O God, give me eyes to see the paradise you have placed me in today.

Give me eyes to see the stars and the moon at night and the rising of the morning sun.

Give me eyes to see your garden of delight.

Give me a heart filled with gratitude for all that you have provided.

Help me to listen to your voice no matter what.

And when I fail, remind me that you want to bring me back to paradise.

Remind me that I can choose paradise, and that is your heart's desire.

Remind me of that way today and forever.

Journal Entries

1. Take the time to describe the paradise God created for Eve to live in. Use your imagination.

2. Describe your own idea of paradise, the one you dream of living in. How is it similar to Eve's paradise? How is it different?

3. What makes living in paradise possible today?

4. When have you exchanged God's truth for a lie?

5. What were the results?

6. How is Eve's story your story?

Scripture References

Genesis 2 and 3; 2 Corinthians 11:3

Looking Back

"But Lot's wife looked back, and
she became a pillar of salt."
(Gen. 19:26)

I would not describe myself as a woman who
looks back. After I graduated from Stephen D. Lee High
School in 1961, I didn't look back in the sense of wanting to do it all over again. I didn't want to be that age
again or do those things again in quite the same way. I
was ready to do things differently. And the same was true
for me after college. Although it was a great four-year
period, after I graduated I didn't want to go back. There
was something else that I wanted to do then, some other
place that I wanted to be.

I'm not saying that I haven't had nostalgic feelings
for past places and events. I have. When I remember my
childhood, for instance, I love to mentally revisit my
Uncle Tom and Aunt Edna's farm just one more time. I
climb up into the cherry tree outside their kitchen win-
dow and eat fresh cherries, or I pick ripe muscadines from
the vine, drink homemade apple cider, or eat fresh homemade biscuits with steak on a Sunday morning. I sleep on
the feather bed under a handmade quilt. The more I
think about it, who wouldn't want to return to a place
like that?

While I am a woman with nostalgic feelings for a
particular time and place, I am a woman who also has

engaged in other forms of looking back. I have looked over my shoulder from time to time, unsure of where or who I was in the world for the moment. I have occasionally had thoughts about what might have been. I have engaged in some second-guessing in my life. I have certainly longed for the things of this world and have gone so far as to allow the things of this world to crowd in on me so that I have had no room or time left for God in my life. The cares of this world drowned out his voice, and I paid a dear price.

The story of Lot's wife is an intriguing one. For looking back, she paid the dearest price of all—her life.

When I read the story of Lot's wife, I have to ask myself why it is that she wanted to look back in the first place. For some reason, I try to give this woman the benefit of the doubt, some legitimate reason for looking back. Did she look back actually wanting to go back, or did she look back out of sadness and disappointment and loss? What was it that she thought she was about to lose? What was there in her home or in Sodom that she thought she might miss? Lot was a wealthy man. When he and Abraham went their separate ways, they both had so many flocks, herds, tents, and herdsmen that the land couldn't support both of them. Did she live in a fine and beautiful home in the heart of Sodom, with such an accumulation of fine things that she thought she could never replace them?

The wedding plans for her two daughters may have been pressing in on her. After all, it was a necessity then, for a number of reasons, that a woman should have a husband for survival. Husbands could provide daughters a name and a place in the world with children to care for. She may have been concerned about her own place and identity in society because of her husband's loss of

position or influence in the city. They had been somebody in Sodom. Would they be anybody some place else?
Maybe it was something altogether different from any of
those concerns. Maybe it was simply the magnificent
beauty of the land and the rich fertile plains.

We'll never know the truth of what caused Lot's wife
to look back. The story is not recorded for that purpose
anyway. The story is recorded for another purpose. None
of the reasons for looking back that I mentioned or any
additional reasons that you might think of really matter.

This is all that matters: evil reigned in Sodom. The
men of God who visited Sodom had gone there to check
things out. Was this a city that deserved to die? Could
God withhold his fire and brimstone? Was it really as bad
as they had heard? It didn't take long for these men to
find out. They spent the night at Lot's house. During the
night the men of the city, old men and young men .
steeped in sin, attempted to sexually assault them and
would have, had these men of God not struck them
blind so that they were unable to find the door handle.
That incident sealed the fate for the city of Sodom.

These men of God said to Lot, "Get out of here
quick because we are going to destroy this place. We
have been sent here by God" (Gen. 19:12–13 paraphrase). Now we might think that would be all Lot
needed to hear, but he was determined to have his own
way. Lot thought he knew best; he trusted more in his
own judgment than God's. His Uncle Abraham had
already saved his life, literally, and now God, basically
because of his love and covenant with Abraham, was
trying to save his life again. However, Lot didn't quite
get it.

While the men of God were telling Lot to gather up
his wife and his daughters and any other family members

in the city, Lot hesitated. Lot paused to think about it. These men of God literally had to take Lot and his family by the hand and drag them out of sin city. Incredible! God was merciful indeed to this family.

Now pay careful attention to this next scene in the story. The very next words these men of God said to Lot and his wife and the others were, "Flee for your lives! Don't look back, and don't stop anywhere in the plain!" (v. 17). That's clear enough. I think by now I would have gotten the message. But stubborn, fearful Lot didn't. He still insisted on fleeing to safety in his own way. The mountains were too far away, he thought, so he decided to run to a nearby small town called Zoar. "OK, you can do that," the men replied, "but do it fast" (vv. 21–22 paraphrase).

Apparently, Lot and his family ran all day and all night, from the early dawn of one day to dawn the next. As the sun came up, out of the heavens God rained down burning sulphur on the cities of Sodom and Gomorrah and all the surrounding plains, on all of the people of the cities and on all of the plant life.

This was the moment that Lot's wife looked back. It's hard to believe, isn't it? She had heard the message clearly, "Run for your life! Don't look back." This message came from two men of God who had struck the men of Sodom as blind as bats so they couldn't find the door handle to her house. The message came from the men who had physically dragged them out of the city to save their lives.

Maybe Lot's wife was a lot like Lot! She hesitated in her heart. She thought that maybe what these men had said did not really matter. Lot had been spared because of the goodness of God time after time. Maybe God would still spare her in spite of what these men said.

Lot's wife started looking back and second-guessing. *What does that mean anyway, "Don't look back"? That's the city where I've lived all these years with my family. I have a house there. I have friends there. My future sons-in-law are still there.* I hate to think that the lure of sin was in her heart, but it may have had such a grip on her that she had a hard time leaving it behind. Not that I know her sins. I don't. I don't know her lifestyle. Somehow, though, she had gotten to the place in life where it didn't matter what God said. There was a loophole somewhere, some way to get around it.

While Lot's wife was second-guessing and looking back, God said to her, "Don't ask questions. Just listen to me! Don't listen to what your misery or your change in circumstances or your losses or what 1,001 other things may be saying to your mind. Just listen to me and do what I say. I'll save you if you'll let me. I'll take you out of the city of sin by force if I have to. I'll send someone to drag you away, but when I send word to you from men who have risked their lives for you, don't treat what they have to say lightly. Listen to them. Then do it. Just do it."

Eighteenth-century poet William Wordsworth penned a poem entitled "The World Is Too Much with Us." During an encroaching industrial age, which was sucking the spiritual fervor out of him and those around him, he wrote, "We have given our hearts away." That's what Lot's wife did. She sold out. She sold her soul for one look back at a life that was going nowhere. Lot's wife was so wrapped up in her world that she lost sight of God. The world was too much with her in heart, soul, and mind. She couldn't quite let go of it all and say that God was enough.

It's quite easy for those of us reading the story of Lot's wife to shake our heads and say to ourselves, "How could she?" Could we reframe the question with a bit more honesty and ask ourselves, "How could we?" In the face of God's loving rescue, in the face of the cross and all of its glorious implications for the days of our lives, how could we? We hear the imploring voice of God calling, "Come!" and still we turn wistfully back to the world as though it held some promise of hope or anything at all that could come close to the glorious love of God.

Prayer

Father, how I need you to come close once more.

How I need every day to hear your voice calling me to come with you.

Remind me of your love, O God.

Remind me of the powerful lure of sin.

Give me strength to resist the temptation to look back at the familiar.

Give me grace to receive your good gifts, O God.

Journal Entries

1. Are you a woman who looks back? When? How?

2. Why do you think Lot's wife looked back when she did?

3. Why do you think we dismiss the clear words of God?

Scripture References

Genesis 19:1–29; Luke 17:32

Love at First Sight

*Jacob was in love with Rachel
and said, "I'll work for you seven
years in return for your younger
daughter Rachel." (Gen. 29:18)*

Do you believe in love at first sight? I do. In
fact, I hope it happened to you.

Love is a powerful thing. From the beginning of time,
romantics have searched for that person who was willing
to climb the highest mountain or swim the deepest river
just for their love. And some of them found each other.
When my only daughter married the man of her dreams,
a friend of theirs sang for the opening dance at their wedding reception one of the most popular songs of the day
called "Get Here." In essence, it was one of those I'll-do-
anything-for-your-love kind of songs. I imagine it was the
same kind of song that Jacob sang in his heart the day he
arrived in ancient Paddan Aram and met and fell in love
with a young woman named Rachel.

At this time, Jacob was a man on the run. He had
stolen his older brother Esau's birthright, and Esau
wanted to kill Jacob. Their mother, Rebekah, thought it
was a good idea for Jacob to go live with her brother
Laban for a while and find a wife. It just wouldn't do for
Jacob to follow in his brother's footsteps and marry a
Canaanite woman. Those daughters-in-law had already
caused too much grief for Rebekah and Isaac. Rebekah

59

knew that Jacob would be safe with Laban and that in her homeland he would have a better chance of finding a good wife.

On the way to Haran, Jacob had a dream. He heard the voice of God, the God of his grandfather Abraham and his father Isaac, making this promise, "I will give you and your descendants the land on which you are now lying. . . . All peoples on earth will be blessed through you and your offspring. I am with you and will watch over you wherever you go, and I will bring you back to this land. I will not leave you until I have done what I have promised you" (Gen. 28:13–15).

In this place that Jacob called Bethel, the house of God, he made a vow to God, "If you will watch over me on my journey and bring me back safely to my father's house, you will be my God" (vv. 20–21 paraphrase). Jacob accepted a covenant relationship with the God of his fathers. What wife would he find now to help him keep this covenant?

Quite soon after Jacob arrived in Haran, he met Rachel. It was love at first sight. She was a shepherdess, the daughter of Rebekah's brother Laban. Jacob was so overcome with joy when he saw Rachel that he kissed her and wept aloud. When Rachel's father Laban heard the news of Jacob's arrival, he ran to meet his nephew, hugged him, and brought him home with him. It didn't take long for Jacob to let Laban know how much he loved Rachel.

Oh, the things we do for love. It's marvelous. Whatever it takes to marry the person we love, we're ready to do it. We'll stay up late, drive all night, skip meals, work extra hours, bake cookies, anything.

My mother did a lot for love. Raised in the city, one of four daughters, she had nearly everything she ever

wanted. Her father doted on his daughters, giving them
the closest thing he could to a wonderful life. When my
mother met and fell in love with my father, it was love at
first sight. After they married, she was willing to do a lot
for love. She moved with him to the country where she
knew nothing about farm life, milking cows, or drawing
well water. Not only was she willing to change her way
of living, but she was also willing to leave her family to
go with him. She left her mother and father, her three
sisters, nieces and nephews, and her lifetime friends to
move with my father to a small town in northeast
Mississippi. Theirs was a real love story of going the extra
mile to marry and live with the person they loved for the
rest of their lives.

Jacob's love for Rachel was just as great. He was willing to do anything for her love. He had fallen head over
heels in love with Rachel because of her beauty. "[She]
was lovely in form, and beautiful" (29:17). *I've got to have
her*, he thought. After moving in with Laban and his
family, only a month went by before Jacob broke the
news: "Laban, I'm so in love with your daughter Rachel
that I'll work for you seven years to get to marry her."
Jacob hadn't proposed any easy task. A lot can happen in
seven years. Jacob was serious about Rachel, and he
meant what he said. She was worth a lot to him, and he
wanted her father to know it.

As Laban listened to Jacob, he was thinking about
how he had two daughters, and by custom, the older
daughter had to marry first. It was a matter of family
honor. Laban had a bargain of his own in mind. He may
have wondered at the time just how much Jacob really
loved his daughter Rachel. He seemed willing to do
whatever it took to get her, but was he willing to jump
through a few more hoops than he planned on? Laban

saw a real opportunity presenting itself. This was just too good to pass up. Very quickly he figured out a way to have both of his daughters married to Jacob and to receive from him a minimum of fourteen years of work. The only problem was he had to lie about it. Instead of being honest with Jacob about his plans, Laban deceived him. He could have told Jacob the stakes, but Laban was afraid it would cost him.

Jacob met his part of the bargain after Laban had accepted his offer. He worked seven years for the hand of his beloved Rachel, and, when it was time, requested of Laban, "Give me my wife" (v. 21). Laban gave Jacob a wife, but it was the wrong one. When Jacob woke up the next morning, instead of Rachel lying by his side, he found her sister, Leah, beside him. What a shock! In an instant, Jacob had to face the harsh reality of his own father-in-law's deception.

Now it was Laban's turn to be in the bargaining position. Jacob could still marry Rachel after another seven years of work. These two men knew how to drive a hard bargain. Take advantage when they're most vulnerable. Sound familiar, Jacob? That's exactly the way Jacob had treated his twin brother Esau when he stole his birthright. Now the tables were turned, and Jacob knew what it felt like.

Jacob could have stormed out of Laban's tent. But the things he did for love! Jacob loved Rachel. She was the point of all his hard work. After completing the first seven years of work, he said they seemed like only a few days because his love for Rachel was so great. Maybe the next seven went by just like the first. After all, he didn't have to wait another seven years for Rachel to be his bride. He just had to work those seven years to keep her. So begins Jacob and Rachel's love story.

For years after their marriage Rachel was barren while Leah gave sons to Jacob. On one occasion Rachel flew into such a jealous rage against Leah that she demanded from Jacob, "Give me children, or I'll die!" (30:1). Of course Rachel wanted to be a part of carrying on the family name. Only her husband Jacob couldn't do anything about it. But God could. And eventually, when the time was right, God did: "Then God remembered Rachel; he listened to her and opened her womb" (v. 22). Rachel's first son was a baby boy, Joseph, the son who years later paved the way for all of Israel to grow into a mighty nation in the land of Egypt.

Jacob became a wealthy man in Haran. The time came, however, after twenty years when Jacob and Laban couldn't live or work together anymore. There had been too much deception through the years. God said that it was time for Jacob to return to the land of his father Isaac and to his relatives. It was time for Jacob to keep the vow that he had made to God at Bethel that he would do what God said if only God would keep him safe on his journey and return him to his father's house.

There were no good-byes. Jacob didn't take the time, fearing that Laban would try to prevent his leaving. Jacob fled while Laban pursued Jacob and his daughters and his grandchildren, catching up with them in the hill country of Gilead. There at Mizpah we see Laban in his finest hour. He proposed a covenant of peace between their families. "May the LORD keep watch between you and me when we are away from each other" (31:49).

Jacob's next confrontation was with his brother, Esau. How would Esau receive Jacob, the one who stole his birthright years ago, the one he hated so much at the time that he was ready to kill him? Esau's death threat was the reason Jacob had fled to Haran in the first place.

Jacob prayed for God to save him and his family from his brother. He prepared to pay for appeasement and to give his brother many gifts. In a dream the night before their meeting, Jacob wrestled with God, who changed Jacob's name to Israel. Although he left with a limp, at the place of Peniel Jacob saw the God of his fathers face-to-face.

The next day Jacob considered the safety of his family. To protect his beloved Rachel and son Joseph, he placed all the others in the front and placed Rachel and Joseph last. If anything happened to the others, then maybe Rachel and Joseph's lives would be spared. But there was no need for Jacob to have worried at all. Esau was ready for peace. As he ran to meet Jacob, he hugged and kissed him and together they wept.

After parting from his brother in peace, Jacob arrived safely in Canaan as God had promised him at Bethel. Not long after, God asked Jacob to go up again to Bethel where he repeated his covenant with him concerning the land and his descendants: "A nation and a community of nations will come from you, and kings will come from your body. The land I gave to Abraham and Isaac I also give to you, and I will give this land to your descendants after you" (35:11–12).

As Jacob moved his family away from Bethel, Rachel, the love of his life, died after giving birth to a second son, Benjamin. She was buried near Bethlehem. Jacob set up a pillar there in her memory as a monument to their love.

Jacob did it all for love. Wildly in love with Rachel, he endured it all. He worked for her, provided for her, protected her, mourned her, and memorialized her. What a love story we have between Jacob and Rachel. Love at first sight. Has anyone set up a monument of love to you? Have you set up a monument of love for him? Have you done it all for love?

That's our love story with Jesus. Love at first sight. He was willing to do far more than climb the highest mountain or swim the deepest river. He was willing to provide for us and protect us all the days of our lives. Just as surely as Jacob meant what he said to Laban when he asked permission to marry Rachel, Jesus meant what he said when he said he loved us and was willing to do whatever it took to show his love. He gave it all! He gave his life.

Do you have someone in your life like Jacob who loves you as much as he loved Rachel? I hope you do. I hope you're married to someone like that. Whether you are or not, I want to remind you that you do have someone in your life who is willing to go far beyond climbing mountains and swimming rivers. He was willing to spill his blood and breathe his last breath in memory of his love for you. And the pillar that he set up was a cross. With your name in his heart and his arms stretched out in love, he proclaimed before the whole world, "I love you."

When you think of Rachel's love story, let it remind you of your own!

Prayer

O Lord, thank you for telling me and showing me how much you love me.

When I remember Rachel's love story with Jacob, help me to remember my love story with you.

Journal Entries

1. Do you believe in love at first sight?

2. Has it happened to you or to anyone you know?

3. Describe your own love story with God. When did you meet for the first time? What were you like? What was God like? Have you changed?

Scripture References

Genesis 29; 30; 35:19; 48:7; Ruth 4:11

Leah
_____

Loved Less

"Jacob lay with Rachel also, and
he loved Rachel more than
Leah." (Gen. 29:30)

Recorded in the Old Testament is the story of
a woman who sits quietly beside the life of the famous
patriarch Jacob. Against the turbulent drama of this
man's life, we see glimpses of a woman who lived in his
shadow. It is the story of Jacob's wife Leah.

Many of us would rather skip over Leah's life story
because of this simple but painful statement, "[Jacob]
loved Rachel more than Leah." In this ancient story, we
find that one sister is loved more and the other is loved
less. The central truth in Leah's story is the core issue of
our own life stories: recognizing our need to be deeply
and lavishly loved.

The story begins with Jacob on the run. He has
deceived his father Isaac with the help of his mother
Rebekah and stolen his older brother's birthright and
blessing. Because Esau wants to kill Jacob, Isaac and
Rebekah advise him to seek refuge in Paddan Aram with
Rebekah's brother, Laban, and to choose a wife from
among his daughters. The first daughter he meets is the
fair shepherdess Rachel. It was love at first sight.

From the beginning Jacob wanted to marry Rachel,
and at first we have a fine love story. There was only one
problem: Rachel had an older sister named Leah, and as

tradition would have it, the older sister had to marry before the younger one.

Jacob bargained with Laban for a dowry worth seven years of hard work in exchange for his younger daughter Rachel. To Jacob those seven years seemed like only a few days, but the morning after his wedding, Jacob woke up to his worst nightmare. As the veil of darkness lifted, Jacob discovered Laban's deception. Laban had switched brides. To his dismay, Jacob discovered that he was married to Rachel's older sister Leah instead of Rachel.

Laban, certain that Jacob would work another seven years for his beloved Rachel, insured himself a double dowry of fourteen years labor for both his daughters. This was Laban's mercenary deception, not Leah's, since she had no choice except to go along with the plan and the pain.

Jacob obviously had his heart set on Rachel from the day he met her. He was in love with her. Leah had nothing to do with his heart's choice. She simply was a pawn in her father's deceptive scheme at Jacob's expense. The writer compared the two sisters—indicating the reason for Jacob's choice—by simply stating, "Leah had weak eyes, but Rachel was lovely in form, and beautiful" (Gen. 29:17).

Leah's eyes may have been her best feature or her worst feature, but the storyteller makes it clear that she didn't measure up to the beauty of Rachel. Later in the story we read this stark, brutally honest statement that reinforces the reality of Leah's life: "[Jacob] loved Rachel more than Leah" (v. 30).

Leah found herself in the difficult situation of being married to a man who really didn't love her, or who at best loved her less than another. She couldn't change her circumstance. She couldn't just pack her bags and leave.

It was the way things were. For all we know, given the times, it would have been far worse for Leah to have remained unmarried and without children than for her father to have given her to a man who didn't love her enough.

Even though Leah knew that Jacob loved Rachel more, her heart couldn't accept the truth. For a while it became an all-consuming obsession in Leah's life to be loved more than she was by her husband Jacob. After the birth of her first son, Leah said, "It is because the LORD has seen my misery. Surely my husband will love me now" (v. 32). After her second son was born, she proclaimed, "Because the LORD heard that I am not loved, he gave me this one too" (v. 33). And after her third son, she said, "Now at last my husband will become attached to me" (v. 34). Do you hear Leah's pain?

We long in vain with Leah for her husband Jacob to love her in the way she desires to be loved and in the way we know she can be loved as a woman. We long for Jacob to love Leah as he loved Rachel. It never happened. It wasn't true from the beginning. Jacob fell in love with Rachel, not Leah.

Why does Leah pull so at our heart strings? Why is it that we want to rewrite her story so that she, along with Rachel, is loved the same?

Leah's story comes just a little too close to home for us to be comfortable because we live in that same place everyday where we also are loved less by someone we hold dear—a parent, or a child, or a marriage partner, or a friend. We want Leah to be loved as much as Rachel because we desperately want that kind of love to be true in our own lives. We want to be loved more, not less. We want to be number one, not number two or three or four. We need all the love we can get to live, and we go through dry spots in our human relationships where there just isn't enough.

Leah's story conjures up the oldest fear in the book, and we begin to smell the ancient lie. We are tempted again to believe the father of lies that we are not lovable and that maybe, just maybe, we are defective to the point that we cannot be fixed nor loved enough. We are tempted to believe that the great storehouses of love in the world are inherited by others who are more beautiful and more deserving. Sadly, we believe it is we who are the impossibility, the exception. As we read Leah's story, for a moment we are separated from the great reality of our lives—that we are deeply and lavishly loved by God—and as we weep for Leah, we weep also for ourselves.

One of the reasons we have the record of Leah's story is to help us stay in touch with the reality of our own lives. No matter what we do or where we go, there will be those in our lives whose love we long for. The longing is so great because the need is so great. In our relationships we cannot control the love that comes into our lives from other people because love is not something that we can force from another. Love is a gift. A divine gift.

For this story to turn out right for us, Leah must be loved. She has to be. Leah couldn't help the fact that Jacob loved Rachel more. She couldn't change it even though she desperately wanted to and tried to. Jacob's lack of love for Leah leaps out at us because it hurts down to the marrow of our bones. We need love to live. Literally. Everybody does.

On the one hand Leah's story is one of heartbreak. On the other it is a story of triumph. If we read her story carefully, we can see an interesting and significant shift in Leah's response after the birth of her last three sons. It seems as though she took a step back, reassessed her marriage, gave herself a reality check, and apparently realized that she couldn't squeeze more love out of Jacob than he could give. She moved out of self-pity into gratitude and praise. She saw more of what she had rather than what she didn't have.

After Leah's fourth son Judah was born, she said, "This time I will praise the LORD" (v. 35). After her fifth son, she acknowledged, "God has rewarded me" (30:18). After her sixth son she said, "God has presented me with a precious gift. This time my husband will treat me with honor, because I have borne him six sons" (v. 20). We have only one hint that Jacob, in the end, did just that—he treated Leah with honor. When Jacob died, he asked to be buried next to his wife Leah with his parents, Isaac and Rebekah; and his grandparents, Abraham and Sarah. Without making more of the story than is actually there, we must at least notice that Jacob was placed next to Leah's body, and not Rachel's.

But this slender thread of Jacob's honor of Leah is not our primary focus. Our focus is God's honor of Leah. The great love story revealed in Leah's life is not her lack of love from Jacob, but the abundant love of God in her life. She may have missed out on Jacob's love, but not on God's. On the one hand, his love seems so matter of course that we nearly miss it. On the other, it is so huge that we cannot.

Through Leah's son Judah the Son of God is born. Love itself enters the world, takes center stage, and rewrites all of history. Lovely Leah with the tender eyes did not go unnoticed by God. God beheld Leah with amazing love. Jesus came through Leah's son. It is interesting that as we look at this young woman's life, we see such a stark contrast between human and divine love. As human beings we are limited in the way we love. But God is not.

To be loved less in one relationship does not stifle the love that is present. Being loved by God has nothing to do with those relationships where we are loved less. To be loved less by another human being is a fact of life. It happens, whether we like it or not. But it does not negate the great reality of divine love. Those kinds of relationships do not have the power to destroy God's love for us. God will get his divine love through to us.

Jesus came. He came in flesh and blood, flesh that was torn for us and blood that was spilled for us. Tears flowed from his eyes, dripped from his feet, and mingled with his blood. That kind of magnificent and powerful love has found its way into heart after heart. Look for those hearts. Ask God to open your eyes so you can see them. As surely as we are loved less by some other human being in our lives, and we all are in one relationship or another, there is someone nearby who loves us more. And they are there by the grace of the one who loves us best.

The deceptive part of this human predicament, this place of being loved less, is for us to draw the wrong conclusion and to believe the original lie that says we are not lovable and the world has a shortage of love. But the "less-loved" relationship is a set-up. We can see it for what it is—that some people love us more and some love us less. That's a reality of life, and nobody can love us the way God does.

Jesus, God's Son who came through Leah's son Judah, knew the painful human experience of rejection by the ones he loved most in the world, the very ones he came to save. There was no human being who loved Jesus the way the Father did, not even his own mother. And in the face of it, he loved all the more. He loved with all that he had, with his flesh and blood and heart and soul, with truth and compassion.

That is the difference between human and divine love. One caves in, turns inward, and believes the lie; the other keeps on loving no matter what. One turns to and adopts a deprived philosophy of "not enough," while the other turns to the heart of abundance.

While it is important to be loved by those we hold most dear in the world—parent, child, marriage partner, friend—it is far more important that we give love. The great gift of our lives is that we get to give love. That is how Jesus loved in the world. God's love is lavish. His way of loving is the standard. Because he so completely loves us, we have plenty of grace to give.

There is no human being in all the world who can fill us up with the kind of love we need most. It's true that Jacob didn't have the kind of love Leah needed, but he didn't have all that Rachel needed either. He responded to Rachel when she demanded sons of him, "Am I God?" (30:2 paraphrase). He would give Rachel all the love he could, but at the end of the day, as good as it was, he couldn't supply it all. He could not supply what was missing in Rachel's life, but God could.

Perfect, completely satisfying love comes only from God. When we receive it, we can begin to see love all around—even in the dry places where we thought we couldn't, even in the lives of those we've been resentful toward. When we receive the love of God, we know everything is all right. Nobody has to run short on being loved because God is never going to run out.

Do you suppose Leah learned to love like that? She seemed to eventually get to the place where she learned the secret: God would provide enough of his lavish love in her life no matter what the circumstance. We know Leah learned a measure of acceptance and gratitude as God poured out his love into her life through her sons. Because of his great love praise came from her lips.

Getting to give love to another human being is the place in life that God calls us to. The best of life emerges from that place, but often it only emerges after we have been buried under enough pain and sorrow that we rise up to a new life born out of God's love.

God hears our cry. He heard Leah's. God—who loves us with a perfect love—is ready, willing, and able to meet our every need, speaking to the deepest places in our hearts in every circumstance of life saying, "Trust me. I am enough, not just for you, but for every man, woman, and child who has ever walked the face of the earth since Adam and Eve in the garden. I can still take you to paradise now, today, and forever."

In Leah's life, where there was a gnawing and painful lack of love that wouldn't go away, God took notice. God was aware. And God did something about it. He sent his love to this young woman. Did you see it? It's OK to look at Leah's pain. It was there. But don't miss her joy. It was there too. While you have your eyes on your own pain, don't miss your blessing through Leah. Through Leah's son Judah came Jesus Christ, the Savior of the world who lavished so much love on a world filled with people dying for love that there is enough for everyone all the time. There is so much love in Jesus that, as his dearest friend John wrote, the whole world could not contain all the books that could be written about him (John 21:25).

Is there a relationship in your life where you are the one less loved? The other person can't or won't love you for who you really are. Then walk through it with your head held high. Accept it. Love anyway. Love regardless. Love for the sheer joy of getting to give love.

If you momentarily fall into martyrdom or self-pity or resentment, don't give up. Keep loving. Love well. Love long as you lie down into the night and as you rise up in the morning. Love because you are loved, deeper and wider and higher and greater and longer than you could ever have imagined in your wildest dreams.

Believe God. Believe that he loves you. Believe that there is no shortage of his love in the world. We are totally and completely and wholly loved for who we are by the one who made us. As we believe in and allow the powerful truth of God's love to flow through our lives, bodies, hearts, and minds, we, along with those around us, experience its transforming power.

"Put skin on your love," we cry. "Give it flesh, and blood, and bones," we cry.

"I have," he answers.

"More," we cry. "Give us more."

And if we cry "more" in the face of God's gift of his Son who is love, how much more do those around us cry the same? "More! I need more love."

And God says, "I will provide." He will hear our cry just as surely as he heard Leah's cry. And he will answer. He will answer with more love.

What a joyful place to live our lives, giving love out of the storehouse of God's love in us. We are called by God to remember and to rest in this truth: We are divinely loved by God, and he supplies us daily with all the love we can possibly hold until the rest spills over into the hearts of others.

There is no greater single threat to our lives and to the lives of those around us, the ones we hold most dear, than the lie that there is not enough love for us in the world. In the threat of our human limitation of loving enough, the great drama of our lives is how the love of God unfolds itself in our lives.

Our feelings of being loved may wax and wane, but the great reality that we are deeply loved never changes.

75

It never diminishes. It is the great constant, the great axis around which we live and move and have our being. It is the great power through which all hearts are changed. It is the way that God continues to work in his world.

Prayer

O God, when I am tempted to drown in my cisterns of self-pity or tempted to believe the ancient lie of the evil one that there is not enough love, help me to believe.

Give me eyes to see your love all around and, not only to see it, but out of a glad heart to sing about it and to pour it out into the lives of those you bring near.

O God, when I walk through the arid places in my life that bring fear and deprivation, help me to be a woman who walks joyfully and confidently in the knowledge that I am supremely, divinely, and passionately loved by love himself.

Journal Entries

1. Is there a relationship in your life where you are the one who is "loved less"?

2. What has been your typical response to this reality of your life?

3. In dealing with this fact of life, where have you placed your heart, soul, mind, and strength?

4. Have you been able to receive the abundance of God's love for you, or have you at times discarded his love or pushed it away?

Scripture References

Genesis 29; 30; 49:31; Ruth 4:11

Mary of Bethany

Open Home, Open Heart

*Then Mary took about a pint of
pure nard, an expensive perfume;
she poured it on Jesus' feet and
wiped his feet with her hair. And
the house was filled with the
fragrance of the perfume.
(John 12:3)*

I'd like to invite you into the first century
home of a woman named Mary: a beautiful, dark-haired,
single, young woman. She knew what was important in
life, how to put first things first. She was a student with a
passion for learning, especially for the teachings of a
friend called Jesus. Sometimes she frustrated her sister
Martha by sitting all day at Jesus' feet, listening and
learning, while Martha worked in the kitchen. Jesus,
however, affirmed Mary right from the start. She had
chosen to spend time with Jesus, and he had assured her
that in the end this was all that mattered.

Mary was a small-town girl. Her home was in
Bethany, only two miles from the holy city of Jerusalem
where all the major feasts were celebrated, and at the
time of Passover, the city swelled to nearly a quarter of a
million people.

She lived with her brother and sister. John, the
writer of her story, tells us that Jesus loved them all, and
that they in turn loved him. It was evident. Jesus in his

travels throughout Palestine, from Galilee in the north to Judea in the south, had stayed in their comfortable home often for rest, for friendship, and for conversation and teaching.

More than likely, Mary witnessed firsthand some of the signs of Jesus. She listened to an excited retelling of the rest of them in her own home from Jesus and his disciples. Mary had heard the story of Jesus changing water into wine at a wedding his mother had catered in Galilee. The joy of it all had drifted down south into her home. As Jesus visited with her, she listened closely to the story of a woman in Samaria who was isolated, alone, and rejected. The life of this woman had changed so dramatically by the life-giving words of Jesus that she had run into her village to tell the people about her encounter with him. Many saw the difference in this woman, and many believed as a result of her testimony. Perhaps Mary was impressed that Jesus would care so much about a woman—an outcast from society that everybody else had shunned.

Jesus' miraculous work in Palestine continued. Surely Mary had heard of the nobleman's young son who in his dying hour came to life at the very words of Jesus (John 4:53).

Everyone had heard of the healing of the man who had been born blind (John 9). When the disciples had asked Jesus whether the man or his parents had sinned, Jesus said to them, "You've asked the wrong question." Jesus taught them to focus on the man's suffering and his need for relief. He reminded them that this man was given his infirmity so that the glory of God might be revealed. He reminded them and he reminded Mary that this man was a miracle waiting to happen. Everyone had heard how the healed blind man stood up to the

Pharisees. Everyone had heard of his words to Jesus when he first saw him with his new eyes, "Lord, I believe. I was blind, but now I see."

Mary had heard about another sign of Jesus. One evening he had taken a few loaves and fishes and had extravagantly fed more than five thousand people with baskets of his love and generosity left over. No one was hungry anymore; everyone was filled to overflowing. That sign would stay with Mary. That one she would place deep in her heart—Jesus' extravagant love with baskets left over, more than enough love for everyone there.

Mary would keep another of Jesus' signs even closer to her heart. She would revisit again and again that miraculous day when Jesus had given her brother Lazarus new life. Jesus had raised her brother from the dead. Mary had heard Jesus tell the people to take off his grave clothes and let him go. Jesus had set him free from the bondage of death. In fact, this raising of Lazarus from the dead had happened a month ago, and people were still talking about it on the very evening when Mary was invited to a dinner in Jesus' and her brother's honor.

Here at the house of Simon, a leper who had been healed by Jesus and was now a believer, Mary would do something unexpected. Here at this dinner she would do something probably no one had witnessed before. Here she would do a thing that would be talked about from that time forward throughout all of Palestine and, eventually, throughout all the world.

But that's not the reason she did it. She didn't do it for the talk. She didn't do it for the show. Not for the applause. Not for what it would get for her in the way of some return, reward, or recognition. There were no strings, no expectations, no agendas, and no manipulation tactics. In fact, Mary did it because she couldn't help herself. She had literally lost herself in her love for Jesus.

79

When we look in on this intimate dinner among friends in the first century, Martha is serving the meal, of course. Lazarus is reclining at the table with Jesus and the others. Everyone is going about the evening's celebration. "Then Mary took about a pint of pure nard, an expensive perfume; she poured it on Jesus' feet and wiped his feet with her hair. And the house was filled with the fragrance of the perfume" (John 12:3).

Could we, just for a moment, let that scene sit for a while in our hearts? There must have been silence. The group must have been stunned. This was so unexpected, so unprecedented. What could anyone say? Yes, washing feet sandled with dirt and fatigue was a familiar sight, but not a foot washing like this one. This one involved such an extravagant quantity of perfume, an entire alabaster jar that might have lasted for a whole year or maybe two. Every precious ounce was poured on Jesus' feet. This was expensive perfume worth a whole year's wages!

Yes, there was one who spoke up insisting that the money could have been better spent on the poor. Judas did not understand what had been done. He had no spiritual eyes to see it. He had walked with Jesus for three years and still missed the point of Mary's gift. He hadn't allowed the signs to penetrate and change his heart. He was imprisoned inside himself.

Jesus defended Mary's action: "You will always have the poor among you, but you will not always have me" (v. 8). He recognized her love. "Leave her alone," he said (v. 7). No one, except Judas, missed the meaning here. Mary probably demonstrated the most lavish, extravagant act of love ever shown to Jesus while he lived on earth. No one had ever done such a thing.

Has anybody ever shown you that kind of love? "No, not quite," you say? Then let me ask you to think again.

Mary was moved by the love of Jesus, changed from her way of seeing in the world to his way of seeing. Love was all that mattered. How we treat each other is all that matters. There would be the ultimate revelation of Jesus' love at the cross, the ultimate sign of his goodness—a dying young man stretching out his arms in love for a dying world. By then, though, Mary was already a true believer.

If Jesus could feed five thousand people, Mary knew he could feed one more. She knew she wouldn't go hungry. If Jesus could enable one lame man to walk, Mary knew he could do the same thing for her. If he could restore the sight of a man blind from birth, he could give her eyes to see as well. If Jesus could give life to her brother who was dead, he could give life to her also. He could set her free from the bondage of herself.

Mary was a believer. Jesus had stood at the door of her home and knocked. Mary had heard his voice. Mary had let him into her house. Jesus had sat in her garden. He had sipped a glass of wine at her table. He had sat with her and others, talking about his mission and laughing with friends.

Mary had done more than let Jesus into her house in Bethany on the road to Jericho, a small, out-of-the-way suburb of a grand city. Mary had heard the voice of Jesus and had opened the door of her heart and let him in. Then the love of God had literally poured out of her life.

That was the difference between Mary and the religious leaders. She didn't do it to show off. She didn't do it for the applause. She did this extravagant act out of a love so deep in her heart that she knew of no other way to express it than to give the very best that she had. She knew of no other way than to love Jesus with all her heart, soul, mind, and strength. When Mary found herself in Jesus, she gave herself in love.

As John writes his gospel, he still can remember what the house smelled like. He was there. The whole house was filled with the fragrance of sweet perfume. The whole house was filled with the fragrance of Mary's love. We know what that kind of love smells like, and we, like John, don't forget it either.

Only the heart can testify to the love of God. Only the heart can say, "Not my way, but yours." Only the heart can give credence to the new life within. Only a changed life can testify to the presence of Jesus within. This was evidenced in the house and the heart of Mary of Bethany. The changed heart is the evidence today.

Jesus stands at the door and knocks. Have you heard his voice? Have you opened wide the door of your heart to welcome him in?

Prayer

O God, give me eyes to see the signs of your marvelous love all around me.

Help me to open wide the doors of my home for Jesus to enter.

Help me to open wide the doors of my heart so that Jesus can fill it to the brim with his powerful love and so that his love can spill out of it into the hearts of others.

Journal Entries

1. How do you think Jesus' raising Lazarus from the dead affected Mary for the rest of her life?

2. What was it that drew Mary to Jesus with such an outpouring of her love?

3. What is it that draws you?

4. Describe a time when the fragrance of someone else's love filled the room where you were.

Scripture References

John 11:1–44; 12:1–8; Luke 10:38–42; Mark 14:3–11

The Most Important Thing

*"Martha, Martha," the Lord
answered, "you are worried and
upset about many things, but
only one thing is needed. Mary
has chosen what is better, and it
will not be taken away from
her." (Luke 10:41–42)*

Most of us like to be in control of our lives or
at least like to think we're in control. It can be a hard
pill to swallow when we realize we're not. It can also be a
real relief. It's challenging to see ourselves for who we
really are, isn't it? It's also challenging to see other people
for who they are, to accept them and recognize the
importance of what they're doing. Sometimes we have a
tendency to think that we're the only ones who are
doing anything important. Then one day we learn a
valuable lesson about ourselves and about another person
in our lives.

Jesus gave a woman named Martha an opportunity to
come face-to-face with her personality. We have two
accounts, in Luke 10 and John 11, of Jesus confronting
Martha and asking her to answer the ultimate question,
"Who's in control?"

Martha was a good person. She had a lot of ability,
knew how to get things done, and ran her house well.
She enjoyed having company in her home, entertaining

85

them, and cooking and serving a delicious meal. Of
course, she spent a lot of time in the kitchen to get all of
that done, and she didn't get to spend a lot of time with
her guests. Martha, along with her brother and sister, had
often welcomed Jesus. There was an immediate connection among them. They loved him, he loved them, and
their friendship grew. He was the kind of friend who
could speak the truth in love. On two occasions, he
spoke the truth in love about the subject of control to his
friend Martha.

The first time we meet Martha, Jesus gave her the
opportunity to face her true identity. As he visited in her
home early in his ministry, Martha, hurt and disappointed, stormed into the room and said to him, "Lord,
don't you care that my sister has left me to do the work
by myself? Tell her to help me!" (Luke 10:40). Calmly,
her friend Jesus made this observation, "Martha, Martha,
you are worried and upset about many things, but only
one thing is needed. Mary has chosen what is better, and
it will not be taken away from her" (vv. 41–42). Jesus
was not berating or belittling Martha. He recognized her
talents and ability. He was teaching her an important
truth about herself. In essence, he said, "Martha, you're
missing out on the most important thing in life—me.
While you're busy in the kitchen making preparation for
the evening meal, you're missing all the important conversation. You're missing what I have to say to you."

We do the same thing. We're busy. We're distracted.
We're doing our important work in the kitchen or some
other room in the house while we're complaining that
someone else isn't there for us, someone else isn't helping
us get the job done—our job, that is. We're too busy for
what's important. We've got the television on or are surf-
ing the Internet, or we've got our heads into a book or

the newspaper, or we're getting ready to go out for the third time this week, or we're talking on the phone or preparing dinner. There's someone in our own homes who's important, and we're not listening to what he has to say. It may be a son who's getting ready to leave on an extended trip, or it may be a daughter who's having another baby, or it may be someone else.

Then again, that important someone in our homes may be Jesus himself. He can't get a word in edgewise because we won't be still and listen. We're too busy. That's what Jesus was saying to Martha—not that her sister Mary was a better person, but that Mary was taking the time to do the most important thing in life. Martha wasn't. Jesus said that to Martha, not to condemn or shame her, but to show her how much he loved her. He was her best gift that day, and she was looking the other way.

Martha had way too much to do. She felt overwhelmed, and she couldn't stop. She was trying her best to direct the evening so that things went well, but she just couldn't get the help she needed from her sister who kept sitting around listening to Jesus, doing the very thing Martha would like to do too. But she didn't have the time to do that because there were all these other things to do, and if she didn't get them done, who would? Oh, how we like to consider ourselves, our plans, and our work the most important in the world.

Mary chose to listen to Jesus and learn. She chose to hear his voice among all the other distractions going on that day. She chose to be still and to sit at his feet. Jesus said to Martha that the thing her sister was doing would last, and nobody could take it away from her. It was eternal. Why was Martha not at Jesus' feet listening to his voice? All we know is that she was very busy. She was distracted with things that were important, but not as important as Jesus. Martha would not be still and listen until Jesus gave her the opportunity to take a look at herself.

From that point on, Martha's faith grew. While she didn't take time for Jesus in his earlier ministry in Luke's account, she began to find the time. Near the end of Jesus' ministry, Jesus gave Martha another opportunity to face her true identity in her relationship with him as he asked her the most important question of her life.

When we read of Martha another time it was not an ordinary day and not an ordinary visit on the part of her dear friend Jesus. Martha's brother had died four days ago. He lay in the tomb, and the mourners had come to comfort his two sisters. Jesus came to provide an even greater comfort. This time Martha didn't hold back. Instead of Mary, she was the first one to run out to meet Jesus. We hear her voice of faith as she said to him, "If only you had been here, Jesus. I know you could have done something about this. Even now I believe that you can if only you'll pray to God and ask" (John 11:21 paraphrase).

Martha had come a long way in her faith and trust in Jesus. Jesus wanted her to take one more giant step in her adventure of faith. Jesus said to her, "Your brother will rise again." That was good news to Martha. She knew and believed that on the day of resurrection that very thing would happen. She listened more closely this time to the voice of Jesus as he continued, "I am the resurrection and the life. He who believes in me will live, even though he dies; and whoever lives and believes in me will never die. Do you believe this?" (v. 25). "Martha, do you believe what I've just said to you? Did you hear me? Do you understand? Do you believe I'm who I say I am— life itself—and that you don't have to be afraid of death?

I've changed all of that. Believe in me, Martha, and you'll never die. I'm the one in charge here. I'm the one in control. I'm everything, Martha. I'm life itself."

What did Martha say? What would you have said? She made the affirmation that we all are asked to make. Whether she completely understood or not, and she probably did not, still she was able to hear the truth and the power in the voice of Jesus. "Yes, Lord," she told him, "I believe that you are the Christ, the Son of God, who was to come into the world" (v. 27). "I believe that you are who you've claimed to be all along."

Following this second encounter with the truth of Jesus, Martha was still Martha. She still concerned herself with the details of life. We see it when she worried about the smell of Lazarus's body instead of the glory of God when Jesus brings him back to life. We see it an evening later when she, still in the kitchen, prepared the evening meal at Simon's house. But something grand had happened to Martha. She was well on her way. She took the time to hear the voice of Jesus. She knew what was important. She accepted the place of her sister Mary and accepted her own place. She knew who was in control. She accepted the place of Jesus as Lord and Savior of her life.

Prayer

Give me the grace and the strength, O God, to face who I really am.

Give me the measure of love that I need in accepting the place of others in their devotion to you.

When I am too busy and distracted, help me take the time to stop and listen to those who need my attention.

Help me to hear you as you speak the truth in love about myself.

When I try to control the lives of others and become consumed with my own self-importance, confront me and remind me that you are in control.

Help me like Martha to learn to take the time to listen to your voice.

Journal Entries

1. What areas in your life or people do you try to control?

2. When have you been too busy to listen to someone important in your own home?

3. What has been your distraction?

4. Have you been confronted with the truth of who you are?

5. Have you taken steps to change what needed to be changed about your relationship to God?

6. How do you listen to his voice?

Scripture References

Luke 10:41; John 11:17

Loyalty

*"Don't urge me to leave you or to
turn back from you. Where you
go I will go, and where you stay
I will stay. Your people will be
my people and your God my
God. Where you die I will die,
and there I will be buried. May
the LORD deal with me, be it ever
so severely, if anything but death
separates you and me."*
(Ruth 1:16–17)

The story of Ruth opens with a disaster—in
fact, one disaster after another. Her father-in-law dies,
her brother-in-law dies, and after only ten years of marriage her own husband dies. At a time in her life when
she may have been tempted to cave in, to give up, or to
shake her fist at God, Ruth did an extraordinary thing.
As a young, childless widow, she made the decision to
stand by another widow, a woman probably twice her
age, who was angry and resentful and wanted to go back
home and lick her wounds and die among friends. One
who had nothing to give Ruth in return for the favor,
not even another son to marry. This older widow was
Ruth's mother-in-law, Naomi.

Now we don't hear a story like this every day. In fact,
we hear just the opposite. We hear the story of rivalry,
competition, and jealousy, but not the love story between

a mother and her daughter-in-law. It's practically unheard of today.

When Naomi pleaded with Ruth to stay in her native land and not to travel the distance from Moab to Bethlehem, Ruth said no. In fact, she was insistent. Her words to Naomi at this time of bereavement in their lives form one of the most profound statements of commitment found in all of the Bible, in all of literature for that matter.

Ruth was determined to care for Naomi, to live among Naomi's people, and even to die with Naomi. There was no changing of this young woman's mind. She would not leave. What would any one of us give today to have someone in our lives who would say to us, "I'll never leave you. Whatever happens, I'll never leave you." That's what Ruth declared to her mother-in-law, and the most marvelous thing about it was she meant every word.

Ruth meant what she said because when these two women arrived in Bethlehem, while Naomi complained, Ruth got to work. Someone had to go out into the fields, an unsafe place where local workers could easily take advantage of a foreigner, and a woman at that. But someone had to take the risk to get food for their table so they wouldn't starve. The work would have been too hard for Naomi, so Ruth went. She hardly rested before she was up and out and gone, working all day long from sun up to sun down in the fields of a total stranger.

Now this stranger was an interesting man. His name was Boaz. He was influential in the town, well known and well respected, a man who treated his workers with kindness. He was kind and compassionate toward Ruth as well, and he took every precaution that he could think of to protect her.

He talked to his workers about how they were to treat Ruth. He encouraged them to include her and to help her—to go the extra mile. He made it clear that no man was to make a pass at her. He made it clear that no one was to take advantage of her in any way. During lunch, he shared his food with Ruth and gave her extra to take home with her. So why did a man with position and influence show such special concern for a woman who, we might say, was from the other side of the tracks?

For one thing, Boaz had already heard about Ruth. Her reputation had preceded her. The people of the town were talking, and what they had to say about Ruth was nothing but the best. Listen to what Boaz said to Ruth the first time he met her: "I've been told all about what you have done for your mother-in-law since the death of your husband—how you left your father and mother and your homeland and came to live with a people you did not know before" (Ruth 2:11).

When Ruth told her mother-in-law that she would never leave, that she'd give it all for her, she meant what she said. Now Ruth was not a hometown girl. She was a foreigner, and she wasn't just any ole foreigner. She was from a country that these townspeople historically despised. She was a vulnerable widow, a woman living in a time when women depended on men, practically for their entire identity. And Ruth had the whole town talking about her. They weren't talking about the fact that she was a foreigner or that she didn't have a steady job. They weren't concerned with anything, it seems, but that she loved Naomi. They couldn't get over the fact that she left it all for this aging widow who had little or nothing to give in return. Ruth was a woman of her word. She was loyal and she was compassionate.

Ruth was a lot like Jesus. She knew his standard. Before Jesus ever spoke the words to his disciples of how to love in this world, Ruth was living out those very words. Jesus said in John 13:34, "A new command I give you: Love one another. As I have loved you, so you must love one another. By this all men will know that you are my disciples, if you love one another." All of the people of this little town of Bethlehem saw the love of God in Ruth by the way she loved Naomi.

Before Ruth faded into the pages of history, she showed an even greater love for Naomi. She asked Boaz to marry her with the specific idea of having a baby who would grow up and care for Naomi in her old age. Boaz was impressed. He knew that if Ruth could love like that, then this was the kind of woman he wanted to spend the rest of his life with. So he did what he needed to do in order to marry her. The whole town cheered, and prayed, and pronounced their blessings on this couple, and Ruth eventually had a baby boy whose very name meant "servant."

Do you know what the women of the town said about this young widow, this foreigner from a country they had despised, who had made a promise of love and loyalty to her mother-in-law after the birth of her baby? They said to Naomi, "For your daughter-in-law, who loves you and who is better to you than seven sons, has given him birth" (Ruth 4:15). Seven was the ideal number of sons to have for an Israelite living in Bethlehem, and these women declared that Ruth was worth a whole lot more.

Ruth won the hearts of the people with the way she loved. She won the heart of God himself and became one of four women mentioned in the ancestry of God's own Son. What a role model! What a way to live in the world.

Prayer

O God, help me to be more like Ruth.

Grow in me a more selfless and serving heart.

Help me to remain faithful to those I love, especially in times of loss.

Help me to see the needs of others.

And when I see their need, give me the courage to act on their behalf according to your will.

Grow a faith in me that prompts love and loyalty to others because of your love and loyalty to me.

Journal Entries

1. Describe the disasters Ruth faced at the beginning of her story.

2. Describe the progression of her response to Naomi's plea.

3. Why did she choose to go with Naomi to Bethlehem? Do you think Ruth had an agenda or anything to gain by going with her?

4. Describe some of the ways that Ruth showed love for this aging widow Naomi.

5. What was the reaction of Boaz and the townspeople to Ruth?

Scripture References

Ruth 1–4; Matthew 1:5

Change

The women said to Naomi:
"Praise be to the LORD, who this
day has not left you without a
kinsman-redeemer. . . . He will
renew your life and sustain you
in your old age."
(Ruth 4:14–15)

My mother is a senior citizen. My father died
more than a decade ago, and my mother lived without
him in the same home that she had shared with him for
fifty years. That's a long time to live in the same place, a
lot of memories to house. But because of deteriorating
health, my mother needed to make a change and move
out of her familiar surroundings into a personal care
facility. Along with my brothers, my sister, and I, she
helped make the painful and difficult decision to leave
her home.

Here is a snapshot of what my mother looks like
today as a senior citizen. At age eighty-three, my mother
is still a beautiful woman. She still cares about her
appearance and what she wears. She still goes to the
beauty parlor to get her hair fixed once a week, and she
puts her makeup on every day. She scoots along in soft,
comfortable, laced shoes that cushion her feet.

Mother's move to a personal care facility has been
good in many ways. Her days are more structured so that

she receives regular, balanced meals and help with regular waking up and sleeping times. She takes her medicine routinely. Because of her new environment, her memory and her awareness have improved. She is brave and courageous. Even in her shyness, she tries to meet new friends and remember their names. She tries to participate in the planned activities of exercise, devotionals, music programs, and day trips. Although she had rather be at her home on Twelfth Street, she is trying to accept where she is and make the best of it.

I'm aware that some senior citizens make the adjustment to a care facility quite easily, but that kind of change can be traumatic at any age for nearly any personality, and life at times can seem too difficult to bear. Who wouldn't want to shake her fist some days and say, "This is not what I had planned on. I need to go back to my familiar home where I feel safe and loved"?

These are the cries of the heart from the time we enter the world: the need for love and the need to feel safe in the place where we live, in our homes. Wherever "home" is for my mother, she is in the place we all are in. She is only in another stage of living in the hands of God. God is aware of my mother. He knows her needs and he does care. Another woman named Naomi faced a far greater change in her circumstance than my mother has faced, and God was as gracious then as he is now to show her his love and care.

Naomi was a senior citizen of another generation who found herself at a crossroads in life. She experienced such a tragic and unexpected change that it brought her to the point of anger and despair. Her story began as a famine swept through Judah, and her husband Elimelech decided to move his family to the country of Moab where there was enough bread. While living in this foreign land, a place despised by Jews, Elimelech died. Soon after his death, Naomi's only two sons died. We have no explanation of any of these tragedies other than the fact that they happened. At the time we meet Naomi, these were the questions in her life: What will she do in this seemingly impossible situation, and who will help her make it through until the very end?

Here is a glimpse of Naomi's circumstance as a senior citizen long ago. She was an older woman with no husband and no sons. Without a husband she had virtually no identity as a woman, and without sons there was no chance to raise an heir to carry on the family name. This was a huge disgrace in Israel. It was a huge tragedy. Naomi had two daughters-in-law, but their best chance for getting married again, for having a home and a husband, was to return to their parents' home. That was Naomi's prayer for them. She encouraged both Orpah and Ruth to take this step.

Naomi hadn't planned on such major tragedy occurring in her life. She hadn't planned on such major change, certainly not at her age. It's clear that when she looked at the reality of her life, she was angry and disappointed over its overwhelming tragedies. She shook her fist at God and asked, "Why me? Why now?" In addition to her honest anger before God, Naomi had obviously spent some time thinking things through. While she encouraged her daughters-in-law to return to the home of their parents, that's all she wanted to do, too, to go back home to Bethlehem. The sight of the familiar would comfort her—familiar family members, familiar landscape, and familiar worship.

Naomi asked for no one's help. She had nothing to give in exchange for their help. No family, no money, no place, no position, no power. She was an old woman whose only desire was to go back home. Perhaps she meant to die there in peace.

Even though Naomi didn't know it at the time, God sent Ruth to be the one to care for and love her until the very end—with no expectations, absolutely none. It was astounding grace, the most courageous act of love, next to Jesus' dying on the cross, recorded in all of Scripture.

We need someone to love us at every age, when we're young, middle-aged, and old. We need a safe place to live and someone to be there to love us until we die. God provided love and a home for Naomi, and he gave flesh and bones to his love in the life of Ruth. He gave life to his love through her life—in her eyes, in her touch, in her companionship, in her work in the fields providing food to eat, in her marriage to Boaz, and in her baby boy Obed.

At the beginning of our story, when Naomi encouraged Ruth and Orpah to return home, Orpah did. Ruth did what we least expected. She made a vow to stay with Naomi until death, no matter what. From that historic day to this day, we still sing about and celebrate her declaration of love and loyalty and devotion to this aging woman who could give her nothing in return.

When Naomi entered the city gates of Bethlehem, she changed her name to "Mara" which meant "bitter." Yes, she had left this place, her home, years ago. She had left it full. Now she was returning empty-handed. She once had a husband, sons, land, position, food, and shelter. Now she had nothing. It is amazing grace indeed to see how God cared for and provided for Naomi at this stage in her life.

The very first thing God provided was a caregiver, a "daughter" with a heart of gold. Ruth knew what to say to Naomi, and she knew what to do. "I'll never leave you," she said to Naomi (see Ruth 1:16–17). She worked in Boaz's fields for their food as soon as they arrived in

Bethlehem. She also knew how to listen. After listening to Naomi's advice concerning Boaz, Ruth said, "I will do whatever you say" (3:5).

Next, God provided plenty of food because of Ruth's hard work gleaning in the fields and the generosity and protection of the landowner, a man named Boaz who just happened to be a near-kinsman. Eventually, God provided Boaz as a husband for Ruth, and he gave them a son named Obed to care for Naomi in her old age and to fill up her earlier loss.

And a family name? Earlier I said the greatest tragedy for an Israelite was for their family name to die out. They were afraid of annihilation. However, instead of becoming obliterated and forgotten about for all time, God cared enough about the plight of this woman that all Israel was blessed through her great-grandson, King David, and all the world blessed through the Son, Jesus Christ.

Does God care about us when we've grown old and lost all that we once had? Does God care about us when overwhelming changes occur in our lives that are confusing and disappointing? Does God care about us when we have no voice, no one to do our bidding, and to listen? The answer is a resounding yes! God knows, cares, and provides. Wherever we are in the world, we can be safe at home with God where we are deeply and lavishly loved.

Today, will he raise up other "angels" like Ruth with arms to hold, with warm bright eyes to love, and with enough heart to care for us until we die? Pray for them to come. Pray that you will be one.

Love and a safe place to be can come in many forms. We can be at home anywhere we might happen to live, and we can certainly be loved by many different kinds of people. My mother is being loved during a hard time and place in life. I pray that she will adjust. I pray that God will keep sending her "angels" to love her and to help her feel safe in this new "home." I pray that at age eighty-three God will give her dry eyes the ability to see his angels and to feel their presence in whatever form they may take, from family to friend or total stranger. Most of all I pray that she will know that she is at home with God wherever she lives and that he will love and cherish and provide for her until the very end.

Prayer

O God, there are times in my life when I face overwhelming change. Help me to remember that I will never go through any change in life where you are not beside me to help until the very end.

Help me to remember that I am at home with you no matter where I live and that my life is in your constant care.

Give me eyes to see the angels that you send my way, all along the way.

Journal Entries

1. Do you know a senior citizen?

2. What major changes has he or she faced? Describe one of those changes.

3. How did he or she handle the change?

4. What "angel" did God send to show his love?

5. How did he or she experience the care of God?

Scripture Reference

Ruth 1–4

Acceptance

*Jesus answered, "Everyone who
drinks this water will be thirsty
again, but whoever drinks the
water I give him will never thirst.
Indeed, the water I give him will
become in him a spring of water
welling up to eternal life."
(John 4:13–14)*

Have you ever felt the sting of exclusion in
your life? Do you remember the occasion? Do you
remember how you felt? Embarrassed, scared, angry, confused, or hurt? We can all probably tap into moments
here and there in our lives when we have experienced
the shame of exclusion and the tremendous need for
someone to love us through it. This story shows a woman
who experienced intolerable rejection and humiliation
for nearly her whole life until Jesus came to her rescue
and let her drink freely from the fresh-flowing waters of
life and love and acceptance.

I grew up in a rather small southern town during a
time in our nation's history when our community toler-
ated segregation between blacks and whites. It was not
acceptable, but accepted. It was the norm, and for a long
while, far too many years, not many of the good-hearted
people I knew said a whole lot about it or did much to
change things.

103

Segregation between black and white Americans living in the South during the 1950s manifested itself in many incredibly dehumanizing ways. Black Americans were given assigned seats in the back of the bus and in the balcony of theaters. The powers that be permitted them to huddle in shanty towns in their own dilapidated houses, their own separate schools, and their own separate churches. Although they were not allowed entrance into any of the restaurants and hotels that white people frequented, blacks were allowed to work in others' homes, washing dishes, making beds, and sweeping floors. While there were too many daily instances of human subordination for me to recount here, one in particular seems parallel to and appropriate for this chapter.

During that period, one of the most humiliating and dehumanizing instances of exclusion came in the form of a single word written on sundry walls, windows, and doors throughout the community. Ironically, in this hot, humid southern climate, it was a word that reared its head near every public drinking fountain. The word was *colored*. A fountain of water, an essential life-giving commodity for everyone in the community, became contaminated by that single, silent, incongruous label. So simple an act as drinking water from a fountain sadly became for many a deadly, daily reminder.

Black men, women, and children knew without any question which water fountain to drink from because somewhere nearby their eyes would meet the word *colored* nailed to the wall. White men, women, and children knew exactly which water fountain not to dare drink from. There was an understanding about it. Society had made an uninformed, misguided decision about who was clean and who was dirty. It was the ugly matter of exclusion.

Over time, things changed. A call went out, and a
dialogue began all over this country about how to treat
another human being. Those who thought the longest
and prayed the hardest concluded that if you love a person or care about other people, you don't treat them like
they're dirty. It's a matter of the heart.

We still need to be reminded today that rejection of
others doesn't work. Self-righteousness doesn't work.
Hatred can lie in the hearts of well-meaning men and
women for years, and the damage can build to the point
where it appears there's no solution, there's no way to do
it any differently. Yet Jesus showed us a long time ago
how to do it his way.

This story describes a woman who was excluded for
years. Others treated her as if she didn't matter, like she
was unclean. She lived on the fringes of society. To begin
with, she was a member of a minority race, the
Samaritans who were despised by the Jews. One aspect of
the extreme disrespect for the Samaritans revealed itself
in and around public places to get water. While Jews and
Samaritans could draw water from the same well, they
were forbidden to use the same bucket to draw with or
the same cup to drink from. And certainly no conversation would occur between a Jewish man and a Gentile, or
Samaritan woman. Jews had written on the walls of their
hearts the word *unclean.*

As a member of the "wrong" race, this Samaritan
woman had known rejection since the time she was a
baby. Having been despised as a Samaritan for so many
years, she looked for love too many times in all the
wrong places—five husbands. By the time we meet her,
even her own race of people had given up on her. There
was rejection all around, from the Jews and from the
Samaritans as well.

With so much tragedy and so much disappointment in her life, she eventually reached the final rejection. She gave up on herself. She avoided being with other women as much as possible. Why endure the whispers any longer? Why endure the sneers and the disdainful looks? Why suffer any more humiliation?

Over the years it had become too hard to stand tall and to hold her head up. She found the shadows less threatening. She lived everyday of her life with reminders all around her that she wasn't good enough, that somehow she had slipped over the edge and had gone too far to ever come back. One of the first-century reminders of this woman's terrible exclusion surfaced through the drawing of water, that essential, life-giving commodity. She wasn't good enough to draw water from the well with the other Samaritan women. She wasn't good enough to use the cup or the bucket of a Jew, and certainly not good enough to greet a Jew.

This story opened on an ordinary day about noontime. The Samaritan woman chose an unusual time to draw water because none of the other women would be there. She went alone in the heat of the day when there was less chance of encountering more humiliation. It was a good place to be because it was a sacred reminder of the past. She drew her water from Jacob's well near a plot of ground he had given to his son, Joseph, and from there she could see Mount Garizim, the Samaritan place of worship. This place, this holy ground, and this well were all important reminders of her own ancestral history.

However, while standing in this sacred place, she must have been reminded of the hatred that still existed between the Jews and the Samaritans. I wonder if the recurring and confusing life-theme of rejection and uncleanness welled up in her every time she drew water.

I wonder if every time she went alone to this sacred place to draw life-giving water, she was reminded that her own life ebbed away inside her.

On this particular day, a certain Jewish traveler asked her a simple question. It was reasonable. He had been walking from Judea on his way back north to Galilee. On this hot day, he needed rest and was tired and thirsty. He had no bucket to draw water and no cup from which to drink. The woman had both. So he asked her, "Will you give me a drink?" (John 4:7). What was so out of the ordinary about that?

First, he was a Jew and she was a Samaritan. No orthodox Jewish man conversed with an "unclean" Samaritan woman, and certainly no devout Jew would even consider drinking from her "dirty" cup. It just wasn't done. It was unheard of. The woman was shocked and confused. *Who does this man think he is, and who does he think I am?* Of course, that was the question Jesus wanted to address all along, and, during the course of their conversation, he did.

By the time she gave him his water and by the time they had their talk about the real water of life, this woman was a different person. She had awakened that morning thinking the same thoughts, going through the same motions of life and work. She had gone to the well for water like she did every day of her life, but this day something different happened. Her life changed.

The writer, John, tells us that after they had their conversation, she left her water jar and ran back to the little town of Sychar to tell the people. This woman who earlier had avoided the crowds now sought them out. This woman who wouldn't talk to anyone before now couldn't stop talking to everyone who would listen about this man Jesus. "Come, see a man who told me everything I ever did. Could this be the Christ?" (v. 29).

Her tone of voice, her words, and her enthusiasm told it all. "This is the one we've been looking for all of our lives. Christ is here. He spoke to me! He drank from my cup!" The townspeople who had shunned her before saw an amazing difference in her. It was so amazing that many of them believed in Jesus before they even came to see him.

This woman was finally accepted for who she was. She was treated as clean for the first time in her life. This man knew all about her life story, yet still loved her. He respected her. "I'll drink from your cup if you'll let me. And I'll give you something you've been looking for all your life." While this woman needed water to live, she needed love more.

Because Jesus' love found its way to her heart, she changed, and an entire Gentile community changed. A spring of love bubbled up inside her that would never run dry. No more need to run to all those wrong places to find love. No more need to hang her head down in shame. No more need to feel despised, rejected, and dirty. *I'm accepted after all. Somebody knows all about my past sin and loves me for who I am.*

One ordinary day this lonely, excluded woman looked straight into the face of Love. She heard his voice say, "I'm the one you've been looking for all your life." And her life changed. His is the voice of Love who says today, despite all the dirt in your life that others have tried to pile on top of you and bury you under, and despite all the dirt you've caked on yourself, "I love you. I always have, and I always will."

His is the voice who breaks down every barrier, every wall of division. His is the voice of cleansing acceptance. His is the voice with an endless supply of life-giving love. His is the voice who erases from the walls of our fearful hearts the word *colored* and the word *unclean*, along with all the other dehumanizing labels we can think of, and writes in their places the word *love*.

No other person can post a sign that determines our real worth. No other human being can determine who is clean and who is dirty or who receives the love of God and who doesn't. From the first century through the twenty-first, when the undeserved and ugly threat of exclusion raises its hand to wound, we can turn away and look, along with this despised Samaritan woman, into the face of Love and hear him say to us, "I can give you what no other person can ever give you and no other person can ever take away. I can quench your deepest thirst and fill you up with my eternal, life-giving love. Come and drink of me."

Prayer

O God, forgive me when someone comes my way and I am tempted to place a thoughtless label before I take a closer look.

Give me your eyes to see each person that I meet so that with my hands and with my heart you can extend to all a cup of kindness.

Thank you for the way you love.

Thank you for not keeping your distance.

Thank you for giving me—with your own nail-pierced hands—the water of life.

Journal Entries

1. Describe a time in your life when you felt the sting of exclusion. How did you feel?

2. Was anyone willing to come to your rescue? If so, describe what that person was willing to do for you and how you felt.

3. Do you exclude others?

4. How can you reach the place of acceptance and forgiveness toward others?

5. How can you accept those who are different without compromising your own beliefs or principles?

6. How do you stand by those who have not yet found God?

Scripture Reference

John 4:1–42

Caught in a Higher Love

"Woman, where are they? Has
no one condemned you?"
"No one, sir," she said.
"Then neither do I condemn
you," Jesus declared. "Go now
and leave your life of sin."
(John 8:10–11)

Adultery. It's a difficult word to say and an even harder act to deal with. I have a friend who told me about the first time she ever heard of an adulteress. It was someone she liked a lot, a very pretty, neatly dressed, married woman with long blond hair who sang in the church choir. As a ten-year-old child when she heard about this woman having an affair, she was shocked and confused. For the first time she had connected the word and the act with a real person. How did this sin fit with this person who smiled at her on Sundays?

The two parties involved in the affair were treated differently. Apparently, the man involved stayed in the community and in the same small church where they had met. The woman, on the other hand, was railroaded out of that little church and out of town into oblivion. My friend told me she never saw the woman again after that, but she has wondered through the years if someone had treated her differently whether she might have made a comeback.

Today, adultery still seems to be that unpardonable place of no return where desperate people have chosen to go. Adulterers have a hard time forgiving themselves, and others have a hard time forgiving them. Too many times the temptation for the rest of us is to nail them, leave them in their unpardonable place, and go on our way. The problem I have with that is this: If I leave one man or one woman in that place, I leave part of me in the same place, and I don't ever want to go to a place from which I can never return to my family, friends, and God. Not ever.

If that is the case with me, it must surely be the case with everyone else. I understand that sin is not something we can gloss over or trifle with. I understand that we cannot minimize sin and its disastrous effects either in our own lives or in the lives of others. How can we remain faithful to the heart of God when we encounter someone who has committed adultery? What would Jesus do? We're not left in the dark about this. Jesus showed us very clearly how he treated a woman caught in the act of adultery.

Jesus was teaching in the temple when the religious leaders interrupted him. They dragged in a woman who was caught in the act of adultery and forced her to stand before the group. They legalistically tried to set Jesus up: "Teacher, this woman was caught in the act of adultery. In the Law Moses commanded us to stone such women. Now what do you say?" (John 8:4–5).

Entrapment, pure and simple. The text says so. All these religious leaders had in mind was entrapment. Publicly, they intended to use this woman's humiliating sin in order to force Jesus' hand. If Jesus said anything contrary to the sacred law of Moses, then he would lose face with the crowds; and the establishment could rest easy again. With every foiled attempt on the part of these threatened religious leaders, however, the people pressed even closer to this man they called the Messiah.

Here was Jesus' response. Jesus didn't deny the law of Moses. At first he didn't say anything. He simply bent down and wrote on the ground with his finger. There has been some speculation that he may have written down the sins of the woman's accusers. Regardless, however, after he wrote on the ground, he straightened up and said, "If any one of you is without sin, let him be the first to throw a stone at her" (v. 7). Surprise! That's a zinger if ever I heard one. Jesus protected the woman, not the letter of the law. Jesus focused on a person, a human being. You have the right to put this woman to death. The law in Leviticus says that you do. But Jesus appealed to a higher law than the letter of the law. He appealed to the law of love and compassion.

One by one the crowd dispersed. One by one, the older ones and then the younger ones silently stole away, without one word of rebuke. Jesus was left alone with this woman who had been caught in adultery. He asked her, "Woman, where are they? Has no one condemned you?" (v. 10).

Then we hear the first words from the woman as she responded to Jesus. When I try to imagine the tone of her voice, I can almost hear the whisper, the falter. I almost can see the tears in her eyes, the astonished look on her face, and the inexpressible gratitude that someone had the courage and the compassion to stand up for her in her sin and disgrace. "No one, sir," she said. "Then neither do I condemn you," Jesus declared. "Go now and leave your life of sin" (v. 11).

I don't know what the woman did after that. She had a lot to think over. Would she live the rest of her life hiding in the shadows, continuing to live a life of an adulteress liable by law and by conscience to the death penalty? Or would she choose Jesus because of what he said and did? Did she see life a bit differently, a way out of her dilemma? I think she did what the Samaritan woman did. I think she thought she could make a comeback. *If this teacher Jesus stood by me and extended his hand to me, then maybe someone else will do the same. Maybe they can give me the strength that I need to live a different kind of life.*

Have you ever been caught in the act of sin? Being caught makes a big difference. That's when we're forced to come out of hiding into the open and deal with the reality of sin in our own lives. There are lots of ways to get caught. We catch ourselves some of the time. Others catch us. It doesn't matter, though, how or when we get caught so much as the fact that however it happens, Jesus is there with us. He says the same thing that he said then to today's threatening group of would-be stone-throwers surrounding us and pointing their fingers at us. "If any one of you is without sin, let him be the first to throw a stone at her" (v. 7).

What matters in the end is our response to the love of Jesus as he stands beside us, not condoning our sins, but helping us see a way out: "Love is the way. I am the way. Leave your life of sin, and come to me."

Prayer

Forgive me, O God, when I hurt instead of helping those who need me to stand by them.

I praise your name that when I needed you most, you were there for me.

I praise your name that I have been forgiven through your sacrifice on the cross.

I praise your name that you have claimed me as your own and that no one can take your love away.

Thank you for calling me to love.

Give me grace to keep on loving until the end.

Journal Entries

1. Why is it harder for people to deal with their own sins before God and easier to point out the sins of others?

2. Is it easier to stand by a friend with secret sin or when his or her sin becomes public? Why or why not?

3. What are some of the ways you can stand by a person you love no matter what until the very end?

Scripture References

John 8:1–11; Matthew 10:42; Mark 9:41

Courage

*"I will go to the king, even
though it is against the law. And
if I perish, I perish."
(Esther 4:16)*

Have you ever had to go out on a limb for
someone you cared about? How far out did you have to
go? Maybe in the process it cost you your reputation, a
huge sum of money, an irreplaceable job, or a valuable
friendship. Have you ever been asked to go so far out on
a limb for someone you cared about that it nearly cost
you your life?

Courage has its price. Surprisingly, it can also have
its unexpected rewards. We never know in the grand
scheme of things what we'll be called on to do, and we
never know—until we're out there on a limb trying to
save a life—whether we might break our own necks.

That's the kind of situation a young woman named
Esther faced when she was only a teenager. Against what
appeared to be impossible odds, she went way out on a
limb, risking her very own life. When the die was cast,
Esther came through—not just to save her own skin, but
to save the lives of the entire nation of God's people.
There have been times in the history of the Jewish
nation when, as a people, they were on the verge of
annihilation. This was one of those times.

History tells us that Esther was the most courageous young queen the Persian Empire had ever known. The preceding Queen Vashti had her own courageous moment in time, but it paled beside the record of young Esther's courage. In addition to her courage, history also informs us that she was the most beautiful young woman in all of Persia. Esther was so lovely that Xerxes, the reigning king of Persia, declared her the most beautiful woman in the entire country when she was only a teenager. What a gift beauty can be! What a spell it can cast. And how God delights in using it for his glory. Esther's beauty won her the powerful position of queen of Persia, but, at the end of the story, it won her far more than personal power. Esther, whose Persian name meant "star," had beauty coupled with courage, a winning combination, and she used both for God in a starring role in history.

Esther's story began as a Jewish orphan. Both her parents had died when she was very young (probably as a result of Babylonian captivity). To rescue Esther from her tragic situation—a young child without a home—her cousin Mordecai, a Jew now living as an exile in the land of Persia, had taken her into his own home and raised her as though she were his very own daughter.

During this period in Persian history, Xerxes, the reigning king, was a poor excuse for a leader of such a massive country. His father Darius and his grandfather Cyrus the Great were generous and able men with vision who had built this vast empire beginning with only a small band of nomads. Xerxes was a great builder also but not a successful military leader. When Xerxes took the throne, he failed to avenge his father's military losses with Greece and only made matters worse.

He appeared less concerned with the people of his country and their welfare than he was with his own excesses. He was rageful, indulgent, and self-centered to the extent of having the queen banished after an extravagant seven-day banquet where he displayed all of his wealth and splendor. Vashti had refused to parade herself before the king and his nobles at his drunken command, and Xerxes' advisors recommended her banishment. Following his ill-advised and rash disposal of the queen, he stayed in a prolonged state of anger and depression for nearly two years.

Knowing that something had to be done about the king's despondency, these same advisors devised a plan to bolster his spirits. The government of Persia would host a beauty contest, commanding the most beautiful young virgin women in all the country to come before the king in the capital city of Susa so he could choose one of them to become his new queen and replace Vashti. While the king's so-called advisors had planned only to bolster their king's spirits and satisfy his sensual pleasures, God had a much larger plan in mind and he used Esther's beauty as a means to accomplish it.

Hundreds of young women came to the king's palace to undergo a year-long beauty regimen. While at first glance it may have appeared to have been an honor for these young women, in reality it was a tremendous sacrifice for them. None of them would be able to return to their homes after having slept with the king. From that point on they were confined to a harem where they would live for the rest of their lives, perhaps never even seeing the king again.

When Esther arrived in Susa, God showed his care for her. She immediately won the favor of the king's servant Hegai, along with everyone else, because of her goodness and kindness. As a result of her noble character, she received special food and special beauty treatments from Hegai, and he placed her in the best quarters available with seven maids to care for her.

By the time it was Esther's turn to reveal her beauty to the king, she was ready. Since it had been three to four years since the probable death of Vashti, the king was ready also. After having seen and slept with hundreds of young women, the king was attracted to Esther more than any of the others who had preceded her. He immediately crowned her queen, held a state dinner in her honor, and proclaimed a national holiday for all the people, distributing gifts to everyone.

As a young queen, Esther was not aware of the extreme prejudice against her people. Even though Mordecai had forbidden Esther to reveal her Jewish identity in order to protect her, neither of them could have foreseen how quickly such radical hatred toward the Jews would manifest itself.

It happened when Mordecai, for religious reasons of his own, refused to bow down to Haman, one of the king's recently appointed officials. In retaliation, Haman, a rash and powerful political figure, decided to murder the entire Jewish nation living within the borders of the great Persian Empire simply because they were the people of Mordecai the rebel. With half-truths and a huge sum of money for Persia's war-torn, depleted treasury, selfish and insecure Haman bribed the king into ordering a massacre of an entire race of people. With a roll of the dice Haman selected the day and the month for the massacre, along with the order "to destroy, kill and annihilate all the Jews" (Esther 3:13).

Mordecai went into mourning, along with all the Jews throughout Persia, when he heard of the plot to kill his people. Knowing that his adopted daughter, Esther, was in a potentially powerful political position herself, he sent word to her about this edict for the annihilation of all their people.

How could this young, inexperienced, new queen possibly be of any help to Mordecai and to her people against such powerful political figures? How could she possibly be of any help in changing the law? Once a Persian law was enacted by permission of the king, it could not be changed under any circumstance. That was the law! There was only one way that she could be of help. Esther could go before the duped king and explain the situation. Great risk was involved in daring to go before the king unsolicited. The risk was nothing less than life or death. If the king extended his golden scepter to Esther, she would live. If not, she would die.

Esther had a choice. She could choose to remain silent, or she could plead for the life of her people. Before making this decision, Esther carefully devised a plan by first requesting a three-day period of prayer and fasting on her behalf. Afterward she was willing to go before the king with this courageous resolve: "If I die, I die" (4:16 paraphrase).

Esther didn't die. The most powerful figure in Persia could have pronounced Esther's death sentence in that moment and never looked back. As a new queen, Esther could have been replaced by a thousand other young virgins in the land. But she wasn't. She used her beauty and her position as queen to accomplish before God the salvation of her people. When she stood before the king with her life in the balance, the king extended his golden scepter of acceptance to this beautiful young woman, stating that he would give her anything she requested. He was putty in her hands.

While God gave Esther beauty and courage at a critical time in her life, he also provided her with the wisdom she needed to accomplish his will. Before telling the king her specific request, revealing that her very own life was in jeopardy because she was a Jew, she first extended two dinner invitations to him and his second in command, the enemy of the Jews who had ordered the murderous decree.

It was not until the second dinner that Esther knew the time was right and she finally made her request clear to the king. "Save me and my people," she implored her king. "We have been sold for murder" (7:3–4 paraphrase). With tremendous courage she faced the enemy of her people, looked him in the eyes, and named his offense. "The adversary and enemy is this vile Haman" (v. 6). All of the implications were there. When the queen said, "My people have been sold," the king realized that his queen knew the hideous plot he had helped instigate. He had been duped by Haman. As a result of Esther's willingness to stand up for her people, the Jews, Haman was hanged on the gallows he had built for Mordecai.

Because no Persian law had ever been changed, with Esther's further respectful pleading before the king, he allowed Esther and Mordecai to write a second decree allowing the Jews to defend themselves. Although the original law was still intact, the Jews were allowed to fight back and defend themselves. Instead of their deaths, the decreed day of massacre ended in celebration for all the Jews, not only in the capital city of Susa, but throughout the land. The Jews' sorrow was turned to joy. On that day, the Jews observed a day of feasting called Purim that has been remembered ever since in every generation by Jews.

Esther, a woman who lived centuries ago, has much to tell women of today. Like Esther, we are queens within our own kingdoms. God has called us to our own moments in history. He is calling us to courageously save the day in his name, to go out on a limb for the ones we love most in all the world. He is calling us to give our lives, to take the same risk using the same words that Esther used, "If I die, I die." That was the deciding moment when Esther's life was saved and the lives of all those she loved.

In Esther's recorded story there is no mention of God's name, not once, not anywhere, although his name is implied everywhere. He was the *real* king of Persia. He was the decision-maker, the one in control of the events that took place against such seemingly impossible odds. While it isn't necessary to say the name of God, it is necessary to acknowledge him as the king of our lives like Esther.

For our lives to be changed and for the world to be blessed, we need to be willing to die for God in whatever form that death takes. It will cost us to live for God. Self-sacrifice for the sake of others matters. We are given opportunity in every area of our lives to give to others what they need most: money, time, love, loyalty, position, honor, and a host of other gifts. God made the supreme sacrifice for us. He died for us. Esther was willing to die for him for the sake of others.

Ever had to go out on a limb for others? Ever had to go all the way out? Esther did. And look what happened!

Prayer

O God, help me to be courageous in the face of what appears at times to be impossible odds.

Help me to believe that all things are possible with you. Help me to be willing to go all the way out on the limb for those I love because I love you.

Help me to be willing to give it all for you.

Journal Entries

1. Have you ever had to go out on the limb for someone?

2. What did it cost you?

3. Who gives you the courage you need in the face of impossible odds?

4. What if Esther had refused to take the risk?

5. What steps did Esther take to meet this unexpected crisis in her life and the lives of her people?

6. How does Esther's story foreshadow the life and love of Christ?

Scripture References

Esther 1–10; Luke 1:37; 18:27; Genesis 18:14; 1 John 3:16; John 15:13

Euodia and Syntyche

Conflict

*I plead with Euodia and I plead
with Syntyche to agree with each
other in the Lord. Yes, and I ask
you, . . . help these women.
(Phil. 4:2–3)*

How do you deal with conflict and disagreement?
Many of us don't deal with it very well. And it's not that
we don't want to. More often than not, we don't know
how to deal with it well. We don't know who to ask for
help. We're embarrassed to admit to ourselves and to
others that we have a conflict in the first place. Who is
a source of conflict in your life?

Euodia and Syntyche, two women in the first century—friends and workers with the apostle Paul—didn't
get along. Paul knew it, they knew it, and everybody else
knew it. These women were not bad women. They were
both Christians who lived in the city of Philippi, the
same city where Lydia lived, as did the Philippian jailer.
They may have worshiped in Lydia's home and provided
an important part of the work of the church in that city.

Paul had preached in Philippi on his second mission-
ary journey and had fallen in love with this church,
which supported his work for the rest of his life. Near the
end of Paul's great letter of love and encouragement to
these men and women in Philippi, he mentioned the two

women who were arguing. I'm sorry in a way that he had to single them out, especially because they're women, but I'm grateful that he did. He put his finger on something that many women have a problem with. However, rather than just naming the problem and leaving it there, Paul offered hope and a solution for Euodia and Syntyche— and for us.

Paul didn't tell us exactly what the women were arguing about. I don't know what their point of contention was. I can think of a lot of possibilities, and the things they disagreed over may not be so far from our own areas of contention. Was it over who was more important to the work of the church? Did one of them receive more recognition than the other? Was it over church politics? Was it over doctrine? Take note of this: Paul didn't include what their argument was about. It doesn't matter.

By the time Paul mentioned the two women, he had already spent most of his letter telling the Philippian Christians the things that *did* matter: joy and Jesus and the gospel. I'm sure that Euodia and Syntyche got the message. Just in case they didn't, though, Paul instructed the other believers to help them get along. He hoped they wouldn't stand in the way of the women reconciling and that they wouldn't fan the flame of disagreement.

The easiest thing in the world to do is to keep someone else's argument going. Take sides. Build trenches. Dig in. Do battle and ask who's going to win. Apparently, the argument was not who was right or who was wrong, and it was not winning or losing. Paul's point was that they needed to get along with each other. According to Paul, it was much more important for them to get along than to argue—even if one of them was right and the other person was wrong. Even if one of them had convinced half the church in Philippi that her point of view made more sense, she needed to stop it.

While it's human to have differences, some conflict is a matter of life and death. Paul knew the difference. He was constantly teaching the grace of God in the face of legalists who wanted to change God's grace into a list of dos and don'ts. Here, however, Paul told these two women to ask themselves, "How important is it?" Apparently in this case, whatever their differences were, they didn't matter as much as getting along mattered. Paul realized that these two women could agree to disagree. It was possible for them to respect each other and to get along in spite of their differences.

Rather than confront the problem, we often like to run from conflict or take sides, doing anything to avoid it or keep it going. There are some levels of conflict, some kinds of issues, where we can agree to disagree. This was the case, apparently, with Euodia and Syntyche.

Paul addressed the problem directly. Paul didn't politely request that Euodia and Syntyche get along. Notice the verb: He *pleaded* with them. What was important to Paul was that these women take a look at what they were doing. They were arguing over something that really didn't matter. It was petty in the big scheme of things.

Paul didn't take sides. He didn't need to. It wouldn't have helped. He addressed both women, both sides of the argument. Arguments exist between two or more parties, and it takes effort on each side to solve them. I've known situations where one person was willing to settle a dispute and the other wasn't. It's hard to get along with someone who doesn't want to get along. All we can do is focus on our part in the problem.

If an argument exists, we can blame the other person or we can take responsibility for our part in the problem. Blaming, shaming, criticizing, and judging won't solve problems. They perpetuate problems. We know all the defense language, all the stall tactics: "But I was right and she was wrong," or "I don't want to compromise my convictions," or "If I say I'm sorry, then it'll look like she won," or "Other people will get the wrong idea." This kind of thinking keeps us in the problem, fanning its flame.

Paul named the problem and he named both parties. Both were being held accountable for the problem, and both were being held accountable for the solution. Remember, their problem was the fact that they weren't getting along. This problem was allowing the disagreement to grow so large that getting along no longer appeared possible. This problem was getting in the way of the lives of these two women, getting in the way of the church community, getting in the way of what really mattered. Both women needed to get over it for their own sakes, for the sake of the community of believers, and mainly for the sake of Jesus Christ.

So Paul pleaded with them "to agree with each other in the Lord" (Phil. 4:2). What's the bottom line here? The life of Jesus and his example. His life and death and resurrection were about reconciliation and harmony and peace—not about petty arguments and differences that got in the way of the whole church or that got in the way of the life of Jesus as it was lived out in the hearts and souls and minds of Christians.

He pleaded with these two women to focus on what was important. Agreement. Getting along. And the reason? The Lord. *For his sake, get along. Focus on him and his life, not on your petty, unimportant differences. God is bigger than your differences.*

Paul confronted these two women by name. He identified their problem. He didn't beat around the bush.

And he did it in love: "You are my fellow workers. Your
names are written in God's book of life" (v. 3 paraphrase). He solicits the support of other Christians whose
names are also written in the book of life.

Sometimes when a problem is brought to light, it can
be a shaming thing, especially if nobody knew about it.
But apparently everybody knew about the problem in
this situation. It wasn't a secret. Paul loved these two
women enough to put the spotlight on the problem. He
focused on the reality of the problem. These two women
would have a hard time staying in denial. They would
have a hard time trying to keep the argument going now,
under these circumstances: "This is important. There's a
problem here. Do something about it Euodia and
Syntyche." Paul did not ask the community of believers
to do the work for them. He pleaded with Euodia and
Syntyche, by name, to do their own work around it.
Then he said to the others, "Help them."

Sometimes, very loving friends may be willing to
confront us, as Paul did with these women, about the
problem of disunity. They plead with us to do something
about an unnecessary disagreement. They even go so far
as to encourage others to help out. "Get rid of the problem," they say.

But our response may be, "How do I do that?" Where
do I put my heart and soul and mind that I have been
giving for such a long time to an argument that, in the
overall scheme of things, really doesn't matter? I know
that the argument is a derailment and that I need to get
back on track, but tell me, just how do I get rid of the
problem?

That's what Paul's letter to this group of early
Christians was all about. He didn't leave any of them
dangling about what they needed. He didn't leave any of

them in doubt about where they needed to put their lives—not Euodia and not Syntyche and not any of the others. Christ is the answer. He will provide the needed help.

Do you have a conflict in your life? Ask yourself these questions: How important is it? Is it getting in the way of my life? Is it getting in the way of other people's lives? Is it getting in the way of God's will for my life and his work? What can I do about it? Try not to focus on what the other person may be willing to do because in the end we can't make the other person do anything. The question for us to ask is, "What am I going to do about it?" Maybe the other person is willing to work on the problem and maybe not.

Paul knew that for him and for the Philippians, Christ was the answer. Christ was everything. That's the reason Paul said in the opening chapter, "For to me, to live is Christ and to die is gain" (1:21). Paul had such joy and wanted to give such encouragement because he saw God working in the lives of those he loved. It would be hard for any of us to read Paul's letter to the Christians at Philippi and continue to focus on our problems. It certainly would be hard to continue to argue with a person who loves God as much as we do, a person who wants to serve him as much as we do, and a person that God loves just as much as he loves us.

Paul's love letter puts things in perspective. It's a letter that reminds us of what's really important in life. It's a letter that lifts us up out of the mire and into God's glorious grace. It's a letter that inspires us to do things God's way and not our way. Paul could write a letter like that because he knew what he was talking about. He knew who he was talking about. And he knew why. Always Paul wrote out of a heart changed and moved by the amazing grace of God. Paul was never the same after meeting God on the road to Damascus.

Paul's entire letter was the antidote to arguing. The wonderful beginning to his letter came from his heart: "I thank my God every time I remember you. In all my prayers for all of you, I always pray with joy because of your partnership in the gospel from the first day until now, being confident of this, that he who began a good work in you will carry it on to completion until the day of Christ Jesus" (1:3–6). That prayer from Paul's heart included these two women who were having a hard time of it, Euodia and Syntyche.

Paul continued in his letter with another prayer that included Euodia and Syntyche: "that your love may abound more and more in knowledge and depth of insight, so that you may be able to discern what is best and may be pure and blameless until the day of Christ, filled with the fruit of righteousness that comes through Jesus Christ—to the glory and praise of God" (vv. 9–10).

Paul brought healing and encouragement throughout his letter: "Do nothing out of selfish ambition or vain conceit, but in humility consider others better than your-selves. Each of you should look not only to your own interests, but also to the interests of others. Your attitude should be the same as that of Christ Jesus" (2:3–5). "Do everything without complaining or arguing, so that you may become blameless and pure, children of God without fault in a crooked and depraved generation, in which you shine like stars in the universe" (vv. 14–15).

Then Paul wrote that he had every reason in the world to put his confidence in his own personhood. He was somebody, with place and position and power, cir-cumcised, an Israelite of the tribe of Benjamin, "a Hebrew of Hebrews," a Pharisee.

> "But whatever was to my profit I now
> consider loss for the sake of Christ. . . . I
> consider everything a loss compared to
> the surpassing greatness of knowing Christ
> Jesus my Lord, for whose sake I have lost
> all things. I consider them rubbish, that I
> may gain Christ and be found in him, . . .
> I press on to take hold of that for which
> Christ Jesus took hold of me. . . .
> Forgetting what is behind and straining
> toward what is ahead, I press on toward
> the goal to win the prize for which God
> has called me heavenward in Christ Jesus.
> . . . Rejoice in the Lord always. . . . The
> Lord is near. Do not be anxious about
> anything." (3:7–9, 12–14; 4:4–6)

Come to God in prayer, and let his incomprehensible peace have its way inside of you through the power of Jesus Christ. Fill your minds with what is good and right and true. Paul was saying, "I know what I'm talking about. I've been there. I've learned the great secret to life so that I am content in every situation. I can do it all because of the one who keeps on giving me strength. He has met every need I ever had in life, and he will meet yours as well through the riches of his Son Jesus Christ."

Do you think that Euodia and Syntyche kept on arguing after reading a letter like that? Do you think they were able to put their differences aside or at least in perspective and get on with the things that were important, like letting their lives "shine like stars in the universe" because of the surpassing worth of knowing Jesus Christ? (2:15).

Do you think the other believers offered them help and prayers of reconciliation? Do you think they stopped taking sides and fanning the flame of contention? Do you think that Euodia and Syntyche's arguing stopped the day they read Paul's letter or the day after? Do you think they both found a way to come to the table and discuss their differences and lay them aside for the higher good, for the life of Jesus?

And what about the conflict in your own life? Have you named it? Have you taken responsibility for your part in the conflict? Have you prayed to God about it and asked for his help? Have you asked for the prayers and help of others who care about you and about God's work in the world?

Have you read Paul's letter to the Philippians lately?

Prayer

O God, in the face of conflict, help me to do my part in bringing it to an end for your sake, for your glory. Help me not to be so concerned with the pettiness of being right or the pride of winning that I lose sight of the goal of life.

Help me to believe, O God. Help me to trust that you are on my side and that you will send those who are willing to come to my aid when I need help.

Help me to be willing for you go to the aid of others. Help me to remember the one that you did send—for us all.

You, O God, are the morning sun that shines in the dark places in my life and gives me light. Help me to shine like a star in the universe, not for the brilliance of my own life, but only for the brilliance of Jesus.

Journal Entries

1. Are you in conflict with an important person in your life? If so, is it private or is it something others know about? How much unrest has it caused you or others? How long has it lasted?

2. What solution to conflict has worked best for you in a past or present situation?

3. In your experience, what have you found that consistently has not worked for you?

4. Is it realistic for us to expect to be free of conflict? Explain.

5. As Paul did, have you ever "pleaded" with someone to stop his or her conflict? If so, what was your motivation? Have you seen any results?

6. What has helped you the most in looking at Euodia and Syntyche and the Book of Philippians?

7. What is Paul's answer for us?

Scripture Reference

Philippians 4:2–3

Train Up a Child

*But as for you, continue in what
you have learned and have
become convinced of, because you
know those from whom you
learned it, and how from
infancy you have known the
holy Scriptures, which are able
to make you wise for salvation
through faith in Christ Jesus.
(2 Timothy 3:14–15)*

No doubt you've heard the expression,
"Pretty is as pretty does." As a little brown-haired,
curly-headed girl growing up in the country on the out-
skirts of Memphis, Tennessee, those were a few of the
well-chosen words my Aunt Edna passed on to me. I
heard her say them to me more than once. Are you surprised that they weren't more profound? Well, after
fifty-five years I think I'm just now catching her drift.
As a young child I took them seriously, not just because
my aunt was older but because she was a wise and very
caring woman of God.

Her life was a lot like a silent movie. She said so very
little to anybody, but when her words flashed across the
screen, they counted. They counted for nearly everyone
who was around her: her husband, my mother and father,
my brothers and sister, and me. Her few spoken words
counted because she lived them. We all watched her live

135

them. We knew she meant what she said because the words were born in her heart.

True beauty does come from within. Those five little words, "Pretty is as pretty does," are based in the heart of Scripture (see 1 Pet. 3:3–4). I have little doubt that my Aunt Edna heard those same words from her aunt or her mother. Beauty comes from a heart touched by the heart of God. That was her way of passing on God's truth to a little girl. She passed it on in other ways too. Often by talking to the neighbors who came to buy her fresh eggs or butter or milk, she relayed truths about God's love.

Her picture sits in my kitchen now on a brick counter near my stove. It's a fitting place for a woman who knew a life of hard work and austerity and who spent hours near the stove in her own kitchen. I remember seeing her there as often as any other room in her home, working in silence, baking cornbread or biscuits, churning butter, or mixing leftovers for her collage of hungry stray dogs. When I look at her picture today, I see as beautiful a woman as I've ever known. She loved God enough to point the people around her to him and not to herself.

God pursued me through the love of my aunt. Through her life, he pursued my father as well, and through my father's life, God continued to pursue me and countless others. Now that my Aunt Edna has died and I am left with only her memory, I remember most her love for God, and she wanted me to have that love too. Love is the thing that lasts because it comes straight from the heart of God.

Not everyone has an aunt or a mother or a father who moves them closer to God. I have a friend who has told me that she had no one in her immediate family who was able to move her closer to the heart of God. But

there were others outside her family who did. While she
has spent some time grieving the loss over who was not
there for her when she was young, she has begun to
spend more time celebrating those who were. If only she,
along with countless others, had known in their families
the love of an Aunt Edna or a mother or a grandmother.

A young man named Timothy who lived in the first
century probably spent every day of his life lifting up holy
hands to God in gratitude and thanksgiving for two
members of his family, his mother and his grandmother,
Eunice and Lois, respectively. Their names are only mentioned one time in the Bible, in 2 Timothy 1:5.

Paul wrote his dear, rather timid friend Timothy, who
had become like a son to him, a letter of encouragement
and instruction because Timothy was a young preacher in
the early church. As Paul sat in a Roman prison thinking
of Timothy, their travels together, and this young man's
character, he was reminded of Timothy's mother and
grandmother: "I have been reminded of your sincere
faith, which first lived in your grandmother Lois and in
your mother Eunice and, I am persuaded, now lives in
you also" (2 Tim. 1:5).

Eunice and Lois passed their faith on to Timothy.
Can you think of a better gift? God pursued Timothy
through his mother and his grandmother. Eunice was a
Jewish believer who was married to a Gentile, a Greek.
Although we aren't told one way or the other, I'm not
sure that he was a believer. He didn't object, however, to
Timothy traveling as an itinerant preacher with Paul,
telling the world about the love of God. Eunice had a
relationship with her husband that worked. They were
different, but apparently they accepted, respected, and
loved each other. Eunice didn't let her differentness from
her husband get in the way of what was most important.

137

Later in the same letter of 2 Timothy, Paul refers again to Eunice and Lois. He reminded Timothy that he could trust the ones who had taught him the truth of God, "But as for you, continue in what you have learned and have become convinced of, because you know those from whom you learned it, and how from infancy you have known the holy Scriptures, which are able to make you wise for salvation through faith in Christ Jesus" (3:14–15).

In other words, Paul said: "Timothy, you can trust the things your grandmother and your mother told you about God." The only way I know to trust anybody is to see if they do what they say. Eunice and Lois must have lived how they told others to live. Their walk matched their talk.

I've wondered how they did that. They may have prayed for Timothy before he was ever born. They may have sung to him Hebrew lullabies as he went to sleep or as he nursed at his mother's breast. They may have told him stories about all the great heroes and heroines in his spiritual ancestry. How early did Timothy hear about Moses climbing Mount Sinai to receive from God's own hands the tablets of the Ten Commandments? They may have talked about the great Exodus of their ancestors from Egypt. They may have talked about the time God promised Abraham that he would possess the land of Canaan and his descendants would be as numerous as the stars and about Sarah when she had a baby boy at the age of ninety. They may have told Timothy about the time God called Abraham to take his only son Isaac and offer him as a sacrifice. They may have told him the stories of Jacob and Joseph and Joshua, Ruth and Rahab and Esther.

Did they tell him about Mary, the mother of Jesus, and about the angel appearing to Elizabeth and

Zechariah when John was to be born? Perhaps they told him all the miracle stories of Jesus that they could remember. Perhaps they told Timothy about the little boy who showed up with a lunch of five barley loaves and two small fish and gave it to Jesus who used it to feed more than five thousand people. And when the time was right, did they tell him about Jesus' dying on a cross and being raised again, and about those who saw him and talked to him?

Lois and Eunice probably began with Abraham and said to dear Timothy with tears and excitement, "It's all true, Timothy. It's all true! The things God promised Abraham all came true. The Messiah did show up. We do have a Savior after all. We have been delivered from the bondage of Egyptian slavery, but more important we have been delivered from the worst bondage of all: sin and death!" They must have sung to him and told him all the great stories they had read or heard.

Only, Timothy would not have listened to a word they had to say if they hadn't lived it. Timothy listened to his mother and his grandmother, and he watched them from the time he was a baby. They were women close to the heart of God who passed on to him the only way they knew how to live in the world, a life lived in praise and adoration of God who sent his Son to save us all.

These were two ordinary women who had a lot of work to do everyday—cooking, cleaning, washing, and sewing. They had bad days and good days and days when they were so tired they couldn't see straight. They had days when they didn't get along and days when they did. But they didn't let anything stand in the way of the most important thing. They found the time to teach Timothy God's words from the time he was a baby. How young was Timothy when he could first say the name of Jesus? Lois and Eunice may have written the precious name of Jesus in the dirt and let a little boy named Timothy trace the letters with his tiny fingers.

At the writing of this chapter, I have one grandson waiting on his mother to bring home twins. Of all the things I want for them in life, I want them to be lovers of God, faithful followers who stay close to his heart. My daughter already tells her baby boy stories of the Bible and sings "Jesus Loves Me" and "The Wise Man Built His House." She takes him to his own Bible class. He has his own Bible. She's doing all the right things. But she's doing so much more than that. She and her husband made a decision for her to stay home with her little boy and spend time with him. They get up in the mornings and eat their cereal together, and they go down to the neighborhood playground and swing and slide, and they sweep the kitchen floor together and have a grand old time of it. My grandson eats it up. He loves it. When his mother says a thing or two later on about God, he'll probably listen because of who's saying it.

Another grand thing my daughter does is she loves her husband. Of course, they have their different points of view, but they truly and deeply love each other. Two-year-old little boys watch love. They know it when they see it. They feel it in their bones because it comes straight from a place where they have just come from— the heart of God.

"All Scripture is God-breathed and is useful for teaching, rebuking, correcting and training in righteousness, so that the man of God may be thoroughly equipped for every good work" (vv. 16–17). These were Paul's words to Timothy, but these also are the principles of how Eunice and Lois used God's Word to teach Timothy, and it sunk deep into his heart very early.

What kind of young man did Timothy grow into after the loving guidance from these two godly women? When Paul was old and dying in a cold Roman prison far from home, the person he wanted to see more than anybody else in all the world next to Jesus himself was Timothy, the son of Eunice, the grandson of Lois. That tells me that these two women did something right. We all want to be and need to be as close as we can get to people who are close to the heart of God. Those are the ones we miss most when they're gone. Listen to Paul's words to Timothy at the close of his first letter to him, "Timothy, guard what has been entrusted to your care" (1 Tim. 6:20). What do you think he was talking about? What was the treasure worth such safekeeping that had been handed to him? It was the message of the heart of God: the message that his mother passed on to him and that his grandmother passed on to her and that he would pass on when Paul was gone and that others after him would pass on.

As a woman of God, whether you are a young mother, a grandmother, an aunt, or a friend, are you passing on the message that matters more than any other? Are you finding the time and making the time to talk about the words of God? Are you living the words of God? Are you close to his heart because of the difference he has made in your life? If so, then you can't help but pass it on. And he'll help you to do it every day in every way.

My Aunt Edna who passed the message on to me died years ago. Eunice and Lois died nearly two thousand years ago. But each of their hearts' messages of love and hope and faith live on because of the heart of God. He's looking for other mothers and grandmothers to pass the message on today: to guard it as a sacred trust, to sing about it and talk about it, to believe it—and most of all, to live it.

Prayer

O God, help me to teach those you have placed in my care to love you with my words and my life.

Journal Entries

1. Who is the person in your life who has taught you the love of God?

2. What did she say and do that let you know how much she loved God?

3. Have you let her know what a valuable teacher she has been in your life?

4. Is there anyone in your life that you are teaching about the love of God?

Scripture References

Acts 16:1; 2 Timothy 1:5; 3:14–16

A Name and a Voice

*Jesus said to her, "Mary." She
turned toward him and cried out
in Aramaic, "Rabboni!" (which
means Teacher). (John 20:16)*

    In my lifetime I have seen some important
people and witnessed some spectacular events. I have
seen three leaders of the free world. After Lyndon B.
Johnson became the president of the United States after
the death of John F. Kennedy, I saw him at the state
capitol in Nashville, Tennessee, when I was a college
student. I have seen in my lifetime two other residing
presidents of our country: Gerald Ford at a reception on
the campus of David Lipscomb University and George
Bush at a Republican fundraiser. They were powerful and
impressive men to see in person.

    Besides presidents, I have seen celebrated athletes,
movie stars, and musicians. My family and I were part of
the massive crowds who watched Michael Johnson win
the gold in the 1996 Olympics in Atlanta, Georgia. I
stared straight into the violet eyes of Elizabeth Taylor
one night in downtown Nashville, and I often said hello
to Minnie Pearl at a local market before her death.

    In my life I have been an eyewitness to other people
and events more important and impressive from my
point of view than the ones I have already mentioned.
I have seen my husband pray over and baptize our three

143

children. I have seen my two sons win hard-fought state wrestling titles while in high school. I have seen the major milestone of the graduations of my three children. I have danced, eaten cake, and cried after the late September wedding of my only daughter and was thrilled to see the birth of my first grandson. I have watched the disease of colon cancer steal life from my dear father. I have watched the building of my home from ground zero out of the mud into a monument to family. It is the house I have lived in for over twenty years.

I have witnessed exquisite natural beauty in my own backyard and around the world. I have seen a gray, frozen winter miraculously spring into the soft, colorful beauty of early crocuses and buttercups, hyacinths and tulips. I have seen sunsets die in flames across the Gulf of Mexico. I have walked upon a forest bed of blue wild flowers as far as the eye could see covering the hills rising from the edge of Radnor Lake. I have seen above and below the glory of snowcapped mountains in the Colorado Rockies. I have been enthralled by the rocky coast of Maine and the villages of Vermont and entranced by the mesmerizing blue mist rising out of the dark green tree lines of the Smoky Mountains. I have seen maple trees turn into colors of spun gold and red wine.

I have witnessed spectacular events in my life and seen important people. But all of it, the sum total of what I have seen and heard, pales in comparison to what a woman in Palestine saw two thousand years ago.

Her name was Mary Magdalene. If she had any family at all, she left them to follow Jesus. Her name is mentioned by every Gospel writer as one of the women who followed Jesus and cared for his needs with her own money. Luke, the physician, tells us that she had been

cured from seven demons. Mary had been a sick woman
with a disease she couldn't do anything about. She had
been in bondage to the seven evil spirits that inhabited
her body—enslaved mentally, emotionally, physically,
and spiritually by them. She had been possessed by these
demons and suffered severely.

Mary may well have been like some of the other
demon-possessed of her time. Many of them couldn't talk
and some were partially or completely blind. No voice to
be heard. No eyes to see. Even if she could have spoken,
nobody would have listened to her. Nobody would have
cared. She was refuse, someone for the frightened townspeople to wipe their feet on and cast out of the realm of
social acceptance, compassion, and understanding.

Some of the demon-possessed were driven into soli-
tary places. Some were chained hand and foot and kept
under guard. Most had no home to live in, and many
even stopped wearing clothes. No wonder the demon-
possessed who had been set free by Jesus begged to go
with him (see Luke 8:38).

When the religious leaders of the day were at their
wits end, attempting to insult Jesus any way they could,
the worst name they could think of to call him was a
demon-possessed madman (see John 8:48). While these
words weren't true about Jesus, the demoniac part was
true about Mary Magdalene.

She felt the sting of rejection every day of her life.
She was sick. Something was terribly wrong with her,
and the social mandate was out: "Don't have anything to
do with this woman. She is unclean. Stay away." Talk
about having your self-esteem affected. Do you think
there wasn't a day that went by that she didn't want to
be set free? Just like any other woman who has lived in
sickness, disease, enslavement, rejection, or the miserable

145

loneliness of ostracism, she also wanted to be set free from that which was destroying her. She wanted to be loved and accepted and cared for. Mary wanted to know that her life mattered.

Mary Magdalene heard about Jesus. Maybe he had even heard about her and knew that, when the time was right, he would meet her. And when he did, he didn't add insult to injury or shame her or call her evil. Knowing Jesus' history with the sick and the diseased and the demon-possessed, more than likely, he did the same thing for Mary that he did with the others. He took pity and had compassion on her. He understood.

The evil spirits also understood. They knew who was really in charge. When Jesus spoke, they listened. They knew who he was and they obeyed. A day came in the miserable life of Mary Magdalene that Jesus said to the seven demons living inside her, "Come out of her." And they did. And from that day forward, Mary was never the same. She was set free. We have no record that she begged to go with Jesus like some of the others. Maybe she did. We do have record of the fact that wherever Jesus was, Mary also was there.

She followed him from Galilee to Judea taking care of his needs. All of the gospel writers record her as one of many women who stood at a distance watching, in horror, the crucifixion of the one who had saved her life. I wonder how she must have felt. John records her station at the crucifixion like this, "Near the cross of Jesus stood his mother, his mother's sister, Mary the wife of Clopas, and Mary Magdalene" (19:25). She stood with Jesus' mother. There's no doubt that she loved Jesus with all her heart, soul, mind, and strength. There's no doubt that as the tears flowed down the bloodstained body of Jesus, tears flowed down her cheeks.

And then it happened! Mary thought she had seen all the stupendous, miraculous events her life could contain—all the miracles of Jesus. But she hadn't. She only thought she had. After the darkest hour of Mary's life—Jesus' death on the cross—his body was laid in the tomb of Joseph of Arimathea. Mary knew the place. All of the writers of the life of Jesus record that Mary was there at the tomb of Jesus before the sun came up to anoint his body with spices. She thought that was the only thing left for her to do.

Mary and the other women with her had been concerned about how they would roll away the heavy stone sealing the tomb. But when they arrived, the stone had already been rolled away. In her fear, she ran to tell Peter and John that someone had stolen the body of Jesus. All Mary had wanted to do was to place the spices on Jesus' body. She hadn't anticipated that someone would have taken his body. And she certainly hadn't anticipated what was going to happen next.

After Peter and John had run to the tomb to see for themselves, they went back home believing Jesus had risen from the dead. They knew Jesus had done what he said he would do. Mary Magdalene, however, stood outside the tomb crying. The body of the one she loved was gone. When Mary looked back inside the tomb just to check one more time, she saw two angels in white sitting where the body of Jesus had been, one where his head had lain, and one where his feet had rested. They asked her, "Woman, why are you crying?" [She said], "They have taken my Lord away, . . . and I don't know where they have put him" (20:13).

Mary turned around at this point, sensing the presence of someone standing behind her. Without recognizing who it was in the early morning darkness and

through her tears, she thought he might have been the care-
taker of the garden and that maybe he had taken Jesus' body.
Mary couldn't see this person very well, but she could hear
the voice. He said, "Woman . . . why are you crying? Who is
it you are looking for?" (v. 15) Then he simply said, "Mary"
(v. 16). He called her name. Then she knew. This was Jesus!
Jesus was no longer dead. He was alive! The first person to
see Jesus alive after his death was Mary Magdalene.

What would you have done at that moment? Mary
wanted to hold on to him for dear life. *Don't leave me. Don't
ever disappear again. I can't bear it.* Then he instructed her,
"Go instead to my brothers and tell them, 'I am returning to
my Father and your Father, to my God and your God'"
(v. 17). Mary Magdalene went to the others with the best
news in the entire world, "I have seen the Lord!" (v. 18).

Mary saw the rising sun that morning. She saw her risen
Lord that morning. She saw face-to-face the same Jesus who
had healed her from seven demons. She saw the same Jesus
that Zechariah had prophesied about thirty-three years
before:

> "Because of the tender mercy of our God,
> by which the rising sun will come to
> us from heaven
> to shine on those living in darkness and
> in the shadow of death,
> to guide our feet into the path of peace."
> (Luke 1:78–79)

Others saw the risen Lord Jesus, but Mary was the first.
This bruised woman, who had been crushed by demons and
set free by Jesus, was the first. She witnessed the event of all
the ages. Nothing in all of history can compare.

Have you seen him? Has he called your name? Has he set
you free? Nothing in your lifetime, no event past or present,
no leader of any country or any celebrity any where in all the

world, will compare to the surpassing worth of having seen and heard the man of Galilee, the Son of God.

Prayer

Thank you, O God, for all of the marvelous wonders that my eyes have beheld because of you.

Thank you that you have called me by name to come to you.

Thank you that I have heard your voice.

Journal Entries

1. Who are some of the important people you have been privileged to meet in your life?

2. Describe some of the important places and sights you've seen.

3. Describe some of the significant events you have witnessed in your life.

4. How do those events compare with Mary's?

5. Like Mary Magdalene, have you seen Jesus?

6. From what demons has he set you free?

7. How have you heard him call your name? What was your response?

Scripture References

John 20:1–18; 19:25; Matthew 27:55–56; Mark 15:40–47; 16:1–11; Luke 8:1–3

The Essentials

*One of those listening was a
woman named Lydia, a dealer in
purple cloth from the city of
Thyatira, who was a worshiper
of God. The Lord opened her
heart to respond to Paul's
message. (Acts 16:14)*

What can you and I make of the brief glimpse of a
person's life? There are those robust highly visible lives
and then there are the quieter ones, those that whisper,
those that remain in the shadows of someone with a
larger life. There are women in my life whom I have
wanted to know better. I have seen them from afar and
noticed them, not that they were intent on being
noticed. They weren't at all. That was my attraction.
They went quietly about the business of their lives,
instinctively doing what needed to be done next. Doing
the essentials.

I have known a lot of women whose husbands have
had the higher profile in terms of visibility, women
whose lives some may have missed. I'm grateful for the
quieter women I have known, whose lives, although they
weren't highly visible, pointed out what was important.
We only get a glimpse of Lydia's life in the history of the
early church. But the glimpse that we are given shows us
all that matters in the end. Her life is recorded in the

151

shadows of the great apostle Paul, a man with the greatest visibility in all of the New Testament except for Christ Jesus. Lydia knew the bottom line in her life. It was God. Who was this woman named Lydia? Luke tells us that she was a worshiper of God.

I have known a number of women in my life who knew that bottom line. Some of them are single, some are married or widowed, some are old, and some are young. I am thinking of one woman in particular who is older than I am by a good many years. She is not an upfront, highly visible person and never has been.

Frances is a widow now. She was married for forty-three years to an attorney who was known throughout the state of Tennessee as a brilliant, capable, kind, and generous man. He called his wife "Sweets" and said on more than one occasion that she was the best thing that ever happened to him. She successfully worked as a legal secretary for many years. She has always been involved in helping others, especially young couples and their families who have come to Tennessee from other countries. She has studied with them, prayed with them and for them, taught them to speak better English, invited them to her home for dinners, and taken them out to dinners, celebrated their birthdays, kept their children, and corresponded with them for years after they returned to their homelands.

Frances never had quite as high a profile as her husband because of the nature of his work, but she has been a friend I have loved and admired for nearly thirty years. She knows what is important. Of all the good things that I know about this fairly quiet friend of mine—and I know a good bit—it is that more than anything in all the world she deeply loves God. She worships him. Every woman needs a friend like Frances.

When I read about the life of Lydia, I come away with the same conclusion. A brief glimpse of a woman who knew what was important, a brief glimpse of a woman whose quiet life emerges against the backdrop of the powerful apostle Paul.

We find Lydia living in the major city of Philippi in Macedonia. Originally, she was from a smaller town, Thyatira, in the province of Lydia where women were known for making purple cloth. Perhaps she was named for that particular province. Perhaps she moved from there to Philippi to strengthen her business. There's just a whole lot more I would like to know about this woman, but as I said, we only see a slice of her life. And what we do see is all that really matters.

It is nearly impossible to write of Lydia's life without also writing about the great apostle Paul. We see her in connection with this giant of a man who moved throughout the Roman Empire preaching the gospel of Christ, the same gospel that changed his life forever. Here was a Jew preaching among Gentiles. At one time in his life he had persecuted every believer he could get his hands on, dragging them off to prison in Jerusalem. That all changed for this religious zealot the day he met Jesus on the way to Damascus and heard these words: "Saul, Saul, why do you persecute me? (Acts 9:4). Paul then traded places, so to speak, with Jesus and suffered in the name of Jesus.

Of all men, God chose Paul to carry his name to the Gentiles and to go before kings and all the people he could reach, telling them that Jesus was the Son of God. God took Paul and washed the scales of legalism from his eyes so that he could see the great reality of the love of God in Christ Jesus. God filled Paul with his Holy Spirit, and he was never the same again. He was on fire for God.

153

From the coast of Antioch, Paul and his traveling companions were sent out on three different, major journeys to tell the story of salvation. On his first trip with Barnabas at a place called Pisidian Antioch, Paul preached the story of Jesus: "I want you to know that through Jesus the forgiveness of sins is proclaimed to you. Through him everyone who believes is justified from everything you could not be justified from by the law of Moses" (13:38–39).

On his second journey, Paul went from city to city strengthening the churches and bringing the good news of Jesus Christ. He was in a little town called Troas when he had a vision in the night of a man from Macedonia begging him to come over and help them (16:9–10). Paul got ready to go immediately. He had no second thoughts. And it was on this part of his second journey that he found Lydia in the city of Philippi, the leading city of the Roman colony of Macedonia. In this setting, along the banks of a river, he unexpectedly met a quiet woman who remained his friend for the rest of his life.

On the Sabbath outside the city gate, on the banks of the river with a group of women, Lydia prayed. Paul went outside the city gate searching for this place of prayer and in the process found Lydia. The message he spoke to this group of women was the same kind of message he had spoken in every synagogue in every city he had entered and to as many groups as he could find, to anybody who was willing to listen. Lydia was more than willing. That's the first thing we discover about her. She, a woman of prayer, had an open heart for God, willing to listen to what Paul had to say about Jesus Christ.

The storyteller Luke initially identifies Lydia with one brief paragraph. He calls our attention to the fact, first of all, that she willingly listened to Paul's message of salvation. Not all of us are willing listeners. Not all of us can actually hear the message. The second thing he makes note of is the fact that Lydia was a dealer in purple cloth, the royal color coveted by kings. She must have been something of a successful business woman with a good reputation. In other words, Luke seems to tell us that she was pretty good at what she did. She was important in her line of work.

The storyteller's signature statement about Lydia's life is not about her work, however. In the very same sentence that identifies her work, Luke tells us something that struck him and that strikes us as even more significant about her. He identifies her as a worshiper of God. She had already made the choice in this large, important city occupied by the Romans to turn her life over to God. She was on the right track.

The next thing we read about Lydia is that the Lord opened her heart not just to listen to Paul's words, but to do something about them, to take action. Now I don't think God is in the business of prying hearts open. He opens receptive hearts, searching hearts, hearts that are ready. Lydia's was ready.

Lydia's heart was so ready that she had no intent of keeping this good news to herself. She immediately wanted to share the joy of it all. She wanted her entire household involved, so she and all the others were baptized. Then she persuaded Paul and Silas and the others to stay at her home for a while. This was not a polite invitation because it was the socially correct thing to do in Philippi. This was urgent. Lydia had a way with words. And even if Paul had given any hint of evasion or resistance to her invitation, we read that she persuaded him and the others to come. And they did!

It was important to Lydia to have these men of God stay in her home for a number of reasons. I imagine she felt so grateful for their work and their message to her about the Son of God that somehow she wanted to show her appreciation. She wanted to provide comfort and food and rest. She wanted to wash away the dirt from their feet after having walked through the dusty paths of Philippi and along the banks of the river.

But I think she wanted more than that. As much as she wanted in some small way to return the favor of such overwhelming kindness, I think she wanted to hear more about the man Jesus. She must have requested, "I've heard this much. Now tell me all you know in the few days that you're going to be around."

Between Paul's first and last meetings with Lydia, significant events occurred that strengthened his message in Philippi. During their stay, Paul and his companions returned to the same place of prayer along the river day after day. One day they were followed by a woman who set in motion a whole lot of trouble. She was a slave girl gifted with fortune-telling, and she made a lot of money for her owners. Only one day as she followed Paul, he cast out the ungodly spirit in her. As a result of her owners' outrage over their financial losses, they convinced the city to turn against Paul and his friends, influencing the authorities to strip them of their clothes, beat them, and throw them into prison with instructions to the jailer to watch them carefully.

With their feet in stocks, Paul and Silas prayed and sang hymns of praise to God at midnight while the other prisoners listened with open mouths. As if that weren't enough, a violent earthquake shook open the doors of the prison and broke open everybody's chains, and the jailer in charge was ready to kill himself because he thought the prisoners had escaped.

Instead, he found himself asking Paul the same question that Lydia probably asked down by the river, "Sirs, what must I do to be saved?" (16:30). Paul said the same thing to this Philippian jailer that he said to the seller of purple, "Believe in the Lord Jesus, and you will be saved—you and your household" (v. 31). Paul spoke to the jailer and his family, and the jailer washed Paul's wounds before Paul baptized them. Then he fed Paul, and the whole house was filled with joy because they believed in God.

Paul and his friends received a Roman escort from the prison by the magistrates themselves, asking them to leave the city. And they did. But before they left this city where the lives of families had been changed by the hand of God, Paul went to Lydia's house to meet and worship and encourage the believers. They had done their work there, or rather God had done his work there after calling Paul at Troas to come to Philippi.

This isn't the last time we hear from Paul about Philippi because he remembers his friends there. Paul wrote his most joyful letter to the Philippians while he sat in Rome under house arrest, reminding them of his love and thanking them for their gifts brought to him by Epaphroditus. Apparently, when no other church supported him, the church at Philippi did. Lydia, successful dealer in purple cloth, was more than likely one of those who supplied for the needs of her brother Paul in his work. Paul closes this letter that found its way to Lydia's house with the words, "And my God will meet all your needs according to his glorious riches in Christ Jesus" (Phil. 4:19).

This story is just a brief glimpse of one woman's life. We can fill in all rest. Look at how Lydia's life affects ours. Today, we are reading the same letter she read from Paul. We are comforted and encouraged and inspired by the same words as she. And it's all because she was a woman who knew her priorities. She knew the bottom line in her life. She knew what was really important. While her work was important to her, to her family, and to the writer of her story, what was most significant in her life was God.

Lydia worshiped God. She listened with an open heart, eager to hear all she could about Jesus. She was a woman of action. She wanted her whole family to know what she knew about God and to hear the fire in Paul's heart. After Paul left Philippi, he continued to stay in touch. Lydia continued to stay in touch with Paul, sending him what he needed in his journey, supporting him in his great work of reaching out to others and telling them what mattered most, helping him with her support to find ready, willing, and receptive hearts. Hearts like hers.

Do you have a heart like Lydia's? Are you a true worshiper? Have you found your place of worship down by the river or in your side yard or in a corner of your house? Have you found a group to worship with—a group to encourage and to be encouraged by, a group to pray with and be prayed over, a group whose bottom line is the same as yours, a group who has decided what is crucial in their lives, a group who makes it possible for the message to go on.

If someone were writing just a glimpse of your life, a paragraph or two, what would he write? Would your life say to your readers what Lydia's life said—that God is everything, that God is all that matters?

Prayer

O God, you know that I allow too many distractions into my life, too much clutter and complication.

It's easy for me to spend my time there and miss my time with you. Forgive me.

I long to worship you. You are my delight.

Like Lydia, help me to remember what really matters in life and to put you above all else.

Journal Entries

1. Describe a person in your life like Lydia. What essentials does his or her life reflect?

2. To someone who may write a page about your life, what would your life say to him? What would the essentials be?

3. Do you have a heart like Lydia's? Are you already a worshiper of God? Are you willing to listen to his message? How will you respond? How will you share it with others?

Scripture References

Acts 16: 9–40; Philippians 1–4

Hoarding Treasures

Now a man named Ananias,
together with his wife Sapphira,
also sold a piece of property.
With his wife's full knowledge he
kept back part of the money for
himself. (Acts 5:1–2)

Hoarding treasures is a hard topic for me to write about. I have to admit that I'm still in the process of trying to be more of a giver and less of a hoarder. Gratefully, I am coming to understand more and more everyday that love is the moving force behind the one while fear promotes the other. One is a matter of faith while the other is a matter of fear. There is an incessant internal dialogue that goes on when we're in the place of hoarding something, anything, for ourselves. We say things like, "If I keep this thing for myself," whatever this thing may be, "then I will be safe and secure." In actuality, the opposite of that is true. It is a true paradox that the more we give, the more we receive. It is a paradox built into our whole existence, even nature itself, that out of dying to self, we receive life. All that I have is not my own. It was bought with a price: the blood of Jesus.

Ironically, when we are willing to let go of the very thing that is most valuable to us—the person, place, thing, or circumstance—then we find the real treasure. We can depend on no thing or no one except Jesus

161

Christ to meet our needs. When I say we can depend on "nothing," that includes the whole list: like money, houses, cars, savings accounts, careers, children, partners, friends, parents, and all the rest. When I hoard, I lose. When I give, I live. That's the principle. From my experience, that is how life works at its best. It's that simple. And yes, I can hear all of the "buts" and see all the arrows targeted in my direction. So I'll say it again. When we hoard, we lose. When we give, we live. And I'm well aware that this is a far easier thing to say than to do. It is a process called trust.

"Here, you hog!" When a childhood playmate persistently asked for a bite of a candy bar, that was the reply. My friend raised her small chin into the air with those three scalding words of self-righteous rejection and nobly broke off the tiniest piece possible, handing it to her waiting playmate. Whether as children or adults, we prefer to view ourselves as givers rather than hoarders, no matter how small the gift or how stiff the heart, feeling more put-upon than privileged in giving to those standing nearby the very thing that we have been so gracefully given.

A woman of the first century named Sapphira hoarded money, just enough, of course, for an emergency fund, but as a result she lost her life. If she could rise up out of her grave in Jerusalem, we undoubtedly would hear her say, "If I had another chance, I'd do it differently."

Sapphira was part of the growing Christian community in the first century. It was an extraordinary time to be alive. The early church claimed space. It was on the move. Things were working. By the power of the Holy Spirit, this group of believers was becoming salt and light in the world. Early one summer after Peter preached his powerful, soul-stirring sermon on the day of Pentecost about the death, burial, and resurrection of Jesus, thousands of men and women gathered in Jerusalem shouted, "What shall we do?" Peter replied, "Repent and be baptized, every one of you, in the name of Jesus Christ so that your sins may be forgiven. And you will receive the gift of the Holy Spirit" (Acts 2:37–38). Three thousand of those men and women believed.

A community of believers formed, devoted to the truth of God and to each other. "They broke bread in their homes and ate together with glad and sincere hearts" (v. 46). The city of Jerusalem overflowed with out-of-town company for the annual celebration of Pentecost, and as a result, the believers sold everything they had for the common good of all and gave to anybody who was in need. By the grace of God, this early community of believers grew into the thousands.

The historian Luke tells us these early believers were "one in heart and mind. No one claimed that any of his possessions was his own, but they shared everything they had" (4:32). The apostles continued to tell about the resurrection of Jesus, as grace abundantly filled the hearts of new believers. No one was needy among the group, and the grace of God showed itself as they sold their lands and houses so that the money could be used for the good of all. The early community of believers was alive and breathing and giving. They were in love with God and concerned about the needs of others.

Then along came a married couple, Ananias and Sapphira. They were professing Christians who wanted to get in on the recognition of giving. They sold a piece of property so that the leaders of the church could use the proceeds for those in need. However, they agreed to keep part of the money for themselves just for safekeeping. Apparently, Ananias convinced his wife that this was the thing to do. She didn't object. She went along with the plan. They threw just a dash of fear into their pot of good intentions. The nature of fear, however, is that it can take on a life of its own. It grows. Their fear grew into a lie.

By the time Ananias brought the money to the apostles, he and his wife had decided to keep their rainy day account just between themselves. They made a decision to lie about it, pretending to give all the money for the Lord instead of part of it. No one needed to know about it. But Ananias had the appearance of a man who was lying, and Peter detected it immediately.

The land belonged to Ananias, and he could have done with it whatever he wanted to do. He didn't have to sell it. And even when he did sell it, he could have used the money at his own discretion. As a man of God, Peter confronted him with the truth, "Ananias, you haven't lied to us; you've lied to God" (5:4 paraphrase). And with those words, Ananias dropped dead. Within the hour he was wrapped in a linen shroud and buried.

Sapphira entered the picture only a few hours later. No one told her about the sudden death of her husband. Her clear intention was to carry out their deceitful plan about their financial gift to the church.

Peter asked Sapphira whether or not the amount was all the money she had received for the land. All she needed to do with such a straightforward question was to give a straightforward answer. All she needed to do was to tell the truth. All she needed to do was to say one word: *no*. Instead, she did the same thing her husband did. She lied. "Yes," she said, "that is the price" (v. 8). It would have been so easy to have said to Peter that she had talked it over with Ananias and that they wanted to keep part of the money for themselves. It seems that honesty would have been such an easy thing. It wasn't for Sapphira.

Perhaps she couldn't see what she was doing, lying to herself and lying to God. She must have thought she could go through the motions that looked good and right to everyone else while she kept her heart in the place of fear. It doesn't work when we give one message on the outside while another one is going on inside.

Like Ananias, Sapphira dropped dead and was buried beside her husband. She lost her life. The lesson is clear. It's not easy, but it surely is clear. It is no small thing to trifle with the love of God, or with his good gifts. I believe this couple set themselves up for instant death. Fear kills. Lying kills. Where there is life, there cannot be death. The two don't go together. They hoarded what God had given them in the first place by claiming his land gift as their own. No doubt they said with their lips that they were believers, that they loved God, but they didn't trust him with all their heart, soul, mind, and strength. They didn't trust him enough to let go of it all.

It is a harsh story, but it's hard to miss the truth of it. Selfish motives destroy. Sapphira's intent was to take care of herself and to appear to be caring for others. She was a lot like another traitor of the first century who lost his life to greed. Just like Judas, her heart was in a fearful place. She had a mixed motive. She wanted to appear as though she were giving her all, when in reality she wasn't. She was holding back. She must have held on to the pagan concept that if she didn't provide for herself, she might come up short. She must have thought that God couldn't supply for her what she needed. So she hoarded part of the money from the sale of the land, *just in case*. "Got to cover all my bases," Sapphira said to herself.

That kind of thinking is not about trust. It is about distrust, the height of deceit. Sapphira's lie began with fear. Fear lives where there is lack of trust. Sapphira was afraid to tell the truth. She feared being left out in the cold if she didn't keep part of the land for herself. She feared a lack of security. What if there were no one to take care of her? Perhaps she feared even God wouldn't care for her like he did all the others. *Not enough care out there for me.* Poor Sapphira.

Here's a challenging question for each of us: Do you have anything in your life that you are hoarding? Be careful. Be honest with yourself. If your answer is yes on any level, it will do you absolutely no good to hoard whatever it is that could be of value to someone else. In the end, it will require your life.

What storehouses of treasure are you holding on to for dear life? Can you name it? Is it your marriage or your partner? Is it your son or your daughter? Is it a house or a car or money? Is it your job or your position, your influence or your reputation? Is it your valuable time or giving care to someone in need?

I need to go a step further and ask an even more challenging question. Is the treasure you are hoarding called *love*? Are you holding on to love, afraid that if you give it away there won't be enough out there for you? We have such a long list of objections. What if the well runs dry? What if the other person isn't deserving? Who's going to take care of me?

Every reader has a storehouse of goods to give away: money, time, love, patience, tolerance, and forgiveness. The question is whether or not we are willing to rise above our fear and trust God enough to give it all away to those who need it most. A person's heart can be a fine place for hoarding good things, but the problem with hoarding, as we have so clearly seen, is that it costs us. It costs everyone around us. And the thing it ends up costing is our lives. What have you stored in your fearful heart that you are unwilling to give away?

I have a dear friend who reminds me that ultimately we will give it all. What or who will we give it to?

Ananias and Sapphira gave their lives over to fear. What will it be for you and me? Will we rise to the height of life and give ourselves completely to the One who fills our lives with immeasurable riches every day? Will we give to all God's children who cross our paths because of the One who gave it all for us? Can we remind ourselves again that we are not our own? We were bought at the highest price.

Let's encourage each other to begin a mining process. Let's encourage each other to look deeply inside ourselves to see if there aren't storehouses of good gifts that have been placed within our care for the very purpose of giving them to those who need them most. Let's encourage each other to rise above our fears and lean on the one who calls us to be like him. Let's encourage each other to remember the highest gift of all, "If I give all I possess to the poor and surrender my body to the flames, but have not love, I gain nothing. . . . Love never fails" (1 Cor. 13:3, 8).

Prayer

O God, show me those treasures in my life that I try to hold on to, that I am unwilling to give away.

Cause me to remember everyday that you have withheld nothing from me.

Teach me to be more like you.

Teach me to search out those who need the good gifts you have so graciously and generously given me.

167

Teach me to trust you so completely and love you so dearly that all fear is gone and my heart's desire becomes one with yours.

Give me a heart like yours, O God.

Journal Entries

1. Identify a few of the treasures in your life that you have stored away.

2. Now, identify the one or ones that present the greatest challenge to you personally to give away.

3. What is your motivation for hoarding or keeping these treasures to yourself?

4. What has been the result of hoarding treasures in your life?

5. What do you think would happen if you let go and risked giving them away?

6. Can you think of any treasure worth having that God has withheld from you?

7. Does that truth change your view of giving? Explain.

Scripture References

Acts 4:32–37; 5:1–11

Giving—One Day at a Time

*"For this is what the LORD, the
God of Israel, says: 'The jar of
flour will not be used up and the
jug of oil will not run dry until
the day the Lord gives rain on
the land.'" (1 Kings 17:14)*

What is it that you need today, that you are
languishing without? Where do you go or to whom do
you turn to get your important needs met? Who turns to
you?

Most of us like to think of ourselves as givers rather
than takers, but however we may prefer to view ourselves, when it gets right down to it, it is not always an
easy thing to actually be a giver. It all depends. It certainly is not easy to give something that we are certain
we are running out of. When a neighbor or a friend asks
for a few eggs or a little sugar or flour, it's quite easy to
give him or her what is needed if we have plenty left
over for ourselves. It's quite another matter to give the
last of the flour or the milk or the eggs or the sugar—and
then another still to give the last dollar or the last ounce
of love. As a friend reminds me, if we haven't already
been asked, one day we will be called upon to give it all.

My father-in-law was a giver. Even if he was running
short of whatever was needed, he gave. It didn't matter
to him. He would literally give anyone the shirt off his

back. He would give anyone the last of anything he had. I don't remember a single time when I asked for his help that he didn't respond, and I called him for a lot of different needs. Whenever my car ran out of gas, I called Pappy. He arrived to help as quickly as he could. "Call me any time," he said. "I'm glad to do it." And he was. He brought groceries over to our house in the snow, saved requested newspaper articles, and supported every sporting event any of his six grandchildren ever had. Pappy just waited for a person to name the need, so he could come running. He became a widower at the age of seventy-two and lived the last ten years of his life the same selfless way, without complaint.

Some of my fondest memories of Pappy occurred at Christmas. Even at eighty-two he got such a kick out taking his grandchildren Christmas shopping, trying his best to purchase the perfect present for each one. But aside from those wonderful excursions, I remember another kind of giving. Pappy cooked breakfast on Christmas morning for over twenty years. It became a family tradition. He set two tables, one in the kitchen for the children and one in the dining room for the adults. He set both tables with everyday dishes, each one a different color, and in the center he placed the pepper and salt, the butter, the jams and jellies along with a bowl of Christmas decorations. His six grandchildren insisted on the same menu every year: scrambled eggs, bacon, hot buttered toast, cereal, orange juice, and coffee for the grown-ups. It was simply delicious because he put it together with such love. It was real soul food.

My father-in-law enjoyed his life as much as any person I've ever known. He enjoyed giving away as much of himself as he possibly could to whoever asked. He was anywhere he could be of help, from church to Civitan, the Boys' Club of Nashville to Big Brothers, the Diabetes Association, Special Olympics, Heartbeat, and so much more. He befriended preachers, toddlers, grandchildren, sons and daughters-in-law, widows, old people, and young people. He traveled around the world making friends and helping people, giving them his time, energy, wisdom, kindness, loyalty, presence, encouragement, and humor.

By some standards he didn't die a wealthy man. He had a bare cupboard in some respects. There wasn't much food in his fridge or much money in the bank, but he had more love than we could measure, a twinkle in his eye, and a smile that wouldn't quit. The more he gave, the more he had to give away. That's how I remember him. That's how my children remember him. He never ran short on what we needed. In the end he gave all he had.

Like Pappy, are you a giver? Have you ever had someone to call you in the night asking for your help?

"I need some of your time."

"I need for you just to listen."

"I need some support or advice, encouragement or direction."

"I need a friend."

"I need a cup of sugar. Do you have any to spare?"

Well, do you? Do I? What is our response?

"I'm tired."

"It's too late."

"Go away."

"No."

Everyday there are people all around us who are in need. Sometimes the need begins simply and grows over time. There are those people, including you and me, who find themselves stranded in a wasteland. They find themselves in a desert needing water, or in a relationship

171

needing love, or in a job needing encouragement.
They're desperate, so they turn to you and me.

Famine comes to all of us in different forms. I've
lived through a spiritual and emotional famine and had
to depend on God to send me someone to help, but
I've never lived without enough to eat. I've seen men,
women, and little children around the world on television who have experienced that kind of desperate
deprivation.

But whether we experience a famine of the heart and
soul or a famine of food, we need someone who is willing
to give to us what he has, what we need. We need someone with enough faith in God to keep on giving until the
very end. We need a Pappy nearby.

Sometimes the person God sends to us is the last person in the world we would expect to come bearing his
gifts. That's what happened to a man of God named
Elijah during a national drought. God sent his prophet
Elijah to a woman, the widow of Zarephath, who lived in
a small town near Sidon.

The situation in Israel was extreme. Throughout the
country there was a famine going on, a famine decreed by
the prophet Elijah because of the wickedness of King
Ahab, the most evil king Israel had ever seen. During
this three-year drought, would Israel come to depend on
God for its survival as Elijah did? For a while, Elijah
depended on God to provide meat from a bevy of ravens
and water from the brook Kerith, but after six months
the brook dried up because there had been no rain. How
would God care for Elijah now? It was time for Elijah to
meet the widow of Zarephath.

Before Elijah entered the town, he saw this woman
outside the city gates gathering a bundle of sticks. "Will
you bring me some water and a piece of bread?" he asked

her (1 Kings 17:10 paraphrase). She responded, "All I
have left is a little flour and a little oil, just enough for
me and my son to have one last meal before we die"
(v. 12 paraphrase). God sent Elijah to *this* widow. This
was a woman who couldn't go much farther down. She
and her son were dying of starvation. There was no extra
food. It was practically gone. Yet this was the woman
that God called to take care of Elijah. It hardly makes
any sense at all.

Then Elijah said to this woman, "Don't be afraid.
Go home. . . . But first make a small cake of bread for
me" (v. 13). At this point in the story, I wanted this
dying widow to say to Elijah, "Read my lips, Elijah. I
don't have anything left. Didn't you hear what I said?"
But she didn't. She listened to the rest of what Elijah
had to say: "This is what the LORD, the God of Israel,
says: 'The jar of flour will not be used up and the jug of
oil will not run dry until the day the LORD gives rain
on the land'" (v. 14). God would provide.

And this widow, who was not even a fellow Jew,
believed. She did exactly what Elijah asked her to do.
And the wonderful result of the union of their faith was
that "there was food everyday for Elijah and for the
woman and her family" (v. 15).

That's a miracle you say! Yes, a miracle. This Gentile
woman thought she had nothing left to give, and she was
right. She was exactly where God wanted her to be. And
Elijah? Here he was having been sent to a poor widow
asking for her last dime, her last loaf of bread, so that he
could go on living. Do you think it required faith on his
part just to do the asking? The situation required huge
amounts of faith on both sides.

But they both were dependent. Totally dependent.
And neither of them had anything but a willingness to

believe. That's all. A person can't fake faith. Elijah didn't know how God would provide, but he knew he would. He knew him well enough. And this widow, who had no previous experience with the God of Israel that we know of, had no other place to go. She had nobody else to turn to for help. So that day she turned to God. And then the next day and the day after and so on. All it takes is one day—turning to God one day at a time. "Give us this day our daily bread." Isn't that our common prayer of faith?

It's important for us to notice that God didn't send a deluge of oil and flour. He didn't stack jars of flour and cruises of oil in her pantry. Everyday this woman had to go to the jar in faith, believing that God would provide. Her faith wasn't in the fact that she had stacks of money in the bank or jars of oil in the pantry. Her faith was in the person of God. Her faith was in the one who provided what she needed. There was enough for that one day. And there was enough for the next day, until finally the woman believed that she was not going to run out of what she needed to live.

What do you need today that you feel like you might be running out of? Is it food? Is it something else? Are you running out of patience? Is it joy or gentleness or loyalty or gratitude or contentment? Maybe it's love. Maybe you think you're running out of love and that you might die of starvation. If God cares about dying widows running out of food in ancient times, he cares just as much about you. Look at this widow again. She believed that God would provide. And he did. One day at a time.

God has stored up all the love that we need for this lifetime and the next. He has stored up all the love that we need for ourselves to live and enough to give away to others. That's the real test anyway, in the face of our pitiful cry, "But God, I don't have enough for myself to live another day. I'm going to die of starvation. I couldn't possibly give this small amount away to someone else who needs it. I'll run out, and then what?" Try it. Just try it for a day, and then the next day, and then the next. Let me urge you to step out in faith, to risk love, to live to give for this day that the Lord has made, and this day only, for this day is all we have.

Everybody needs a Pappy. Everybody needs a widow in their lives like the one from Zarephath. Are you in need? Have you asked God to help you? Look for the person he will send your way. You'll be surprised. When you're ready to lie down and die from starvation, he'll fill you up with all you need for one more day.

God doesn't stop giving the oil of gladness or the bread of life. He fills us up with more than enough to give to the next person who calls in the night or knocks at the door saying, "Help me. I need a cup of water and a piece of bread."

Prayer

Give me this day my daily bread that I might give to others the sweet bread of life that you provide for me day after day after day.

Journal Entries

1. Describe someone in your life who you consider to be a giver.

2. What kind of deprivation/starvation have you experienced in your life?

3. Have you ever thought you might die from lack of love?

4. Who withheld that love from you? Was it someone you loved? Was it you?

175

5. What kind of faith does it require to ask for what you need one day at a time? What kind of faith does it require to receive?

Scripture References

1 Kings 16:29–34; 17; Luke 4:25–26